NO ALTERNATIVE ?

Nonviolent responses to Repressive Regimes

edited by John Lampen

William Sessions Ltd
York, England
2000

QUAKER AUTHOR

ISBN 1 85072 243 9

Printed on recycled paper
in 10 on 11 point Plantin Typeface
from Author's Disk
by William Sessions Limited
The Ebor Press
York, England

Contents

	page
Preface *John Lampen*	v
The Hidden Costs of War *Roswitha & Peter Jarman*	1
A Bloodfest *John Pilger*	13
International Peace Institutions *Kevin Clements*	19
Searching for a Just Peace *Elizabeth Salter*	41
International Criminal Law as a Deterrent Measure *Bernard Hamilton*	47
Sharpening the Weapons of Peace *Philip Wilkinson*	55
On Signs, Signals and Action: pre-empting collective violence *Judith Large*	65
Unofficial Peace Work: some experiences under apartheid *John Lampen*	79
Teaching Peace in a Violent Context *Staff of SEZAM, Bosnia*	91
Working for Political Change *Michael Bartlet*	99
What Can I Do? The place of Direct Action as resistance *Helen Steven*	107
Pacifism and the Real World *Diana Francis*	121
Not too Late to Learn *Paul Oestreicher*	133
Notes on the contributors	137

How can they charitably

dispose of anything

when blood is their argument?

Shakespeare: *Henry V*

PREFACE

John Lampen

Many peace-loving people had a deep feeling that it was wrong to bomb Serbia in March 1999; but they were embarrassed to argue the point because they had no alternative to offer in the face of the violent repression carried out by Slobodan Milosevic's regime. Some felt impotent, others wondered if for once our militarists were right.   One letter to the Quaker journal *The Friend* said that the writer had opposed the "just war" doctrine all his life, but now felt unable to do so.   Yet none of my friends who are experts in peace and conflict studies was in favour of the bombing.   Clearly a book was needed in which people with specialist knowledge examined the whole field of alternatives to a violent response, and set them out in clear language for the ordinary reader.

So this book is not about Kosovo, but on how to prevent the next crisis.   It has four aims.   The first is to describe *the means* which we have (or could have) for responding to repressive regimes—the international peace organisations, the smaller and more specialised groups, local peace activists, and current military thinking on soldiers being used as peacekeepers.   The second is to give us a better understanding of *the processes*—when and why does war become "inevitable"?   what possibilities have been missed on the way to that point?   do we try to estimate the hidden costs of war? do the public media distort what they tell us and collude with those who want war?   The third is to consider *personal action*—how can we express disagreement with government policies and hope to have some effect?   And the last aim is to put these questions into a *moral and religious context*.

The book does not give a clear and simple answer to the question "What else could NATO have done in March 1999?"   Once a crisis has been allowed to develop, the choices are very limited. But did the world need to find itself in such a dilemma?   Peace like war must be prepared for, and some chapters are about prevention, including an article from Bosnia on work to teach children the concepts and skills of peace.   Another discusses the

way we neglect and underfund agencies like the UN and OSCE—
and then wonder why they are ineffective in a crisis. The contrib-
utors have a range of viewpoints which do not always agree with
one another. But I hope that overall they will stimulate the reader
and give a range of hopeful insights, practical ideas, and encouragement for personal action.

I am deeply grateful to the distinguished and knowledgeable people
who immediately and warmly endorsed the idea and, despite the
many pressures on them, agreed to write a section. The Joseph
Rowntree Charitable Trust, the Sessions Book Trust and some
personal friends gave strong financial support which quickly turned
the dream into reality. Sessions of York were the most obliging
publishers one could hope to have.

Humanitarian concern is important. My wife and I work from
time to time in the post-war situation in Bosnia. There we share
our friends' pain as far as we can, and support the efforts towards
reconstruction. But if humankind is to abolish war as an instrument of policy in the twenty-first century, it is not enough to tend
the trauma and damage which already exists. We must find out
how to prevent its being repeated. This book is a small attempt
to change our habits of thought.

THE HIDDEN COSTS OF WAR

Roswitha and Peter Jarman

The "just war" doctrine demands that the harm likely to be done by going to war is less than the harm done by not fighting. But how is the calculation to be made? Roswitha and Peter Jarman, who have worked in post-war situations, look at some of the costs which are not obvious and cannot easily be addressed by reconstruction projects.

An elderly Ingush showed Roswitha his portacabin in the makeshift settlement where he had lived since the local civil war of 1992. She admired the neat order he had created around his hand-made bed. "My wife is ill in hospital, do you have some medicine?" he asked. Roswitha, having none, tried to give him fifty dollars. "No," he said, "I cannot take money," so she slipped the notes into his pocket. Tears poured down his cheeks. "What have I done to deserve this?" he asked, "I fought against the Fascists and received war medals. We Ingush were all deported by Stalin in 1944 to Kazakhstan and had to start there with nothing. When we returned here in 1957 I built a house for my family and then came this war. Who is responsible for it? I have no space in this cabin for my five sons, they sleep wherever they can." He spends his days walking up and down the muddy paths that link the portacabins to secure water and a little food.

He has lived this makeshift life for nearly seven years, and there is little hope that he will die in peace in his own home. Who knows how his sons will make their living? In all this pain and humiliation Roswitha felt his dignity, but he probably only experiences humiliation.

We shall describe some of the hidden costs of war: the effects of destroying societal relationships, the disintegration of the social fabric; the trauma, humiliation, confusion and destitution, the emotional chaos in the physical chaos. Post-war situations occur not by evolution but abruptly and with little warning. Suddenly people face a totally changed environment. Who can take charge in this confusion? The link with the past is destroyed. Uprooted, bewildered by the painful present and faced with a future laden

1

with trauma and fear, the victims have to construct new frames of reference to make sense of their daily lives. It is a heyday for extremism.

The societies in which we normally live give us our status, our roots and the knowledge of where we come from. They provide opportunities that we are more or less free to accept. We feel secure and have trust and hope for the future. A healthy society is like a huge and safe family with some parental guidance and with freedom for personal development. Relationships can be made between ethnic groups without undue difficulty. After war this freedom is destroyed. People are left in an emotionally highly charged state of being isolated from one another and thrust into a void. Depression, drugs and crime are routes of escape.

Wars often end by peacemaking and cease-fires followed by the deployment of armed peacekeepers. However the freezing or postponement of resolving the underlying conflict is another hidden cost of war, with the psychological consequences of the war often creating further barriers to that resolution. We illustrate this through our experience of peoples caught up in the inter-ethnic wars of the 1990's in the Caucasus and the Balkans.

On the North side of the great barrier of the Caucasian mountains stretching from the Black to the Caspian Seas that separate Russia from the Trans-Caucasian republics of Georgia, Armenia and Azerbaijan, dwell many different ethnic groups. We shall refer only to the Chechens, the Ingush and the Ossetes, whom we first met early in 1991 through an exchange of community leaders between the North Caucasus and Northern Ireland. A terrible civil war raged between Russian troops and Chechens from December 1994 to August 1996; the Ingush and the Ossetes supported by Russian troops fought each other for a few days at the end of October 1992 over the sovereignty of a tiny patch of land known as the Prigorodny (Russian—"near to the city") District near the capital Vladikavkaz in North Ossetia. A thousand people were killed, mostly Ingush, and about 60,000 Ingush were displaced forcibly mostly to Ingushetia.

We shall also refer to the Croat-Serb conflict in Eastern Slavonia that began ferociously in the early Winter of 1991 when the Federal Yugoslav army displaced all Croats from the Vukovar district. Eastern Slavonia is now part of the Croatian Republic. We allude briefly to the Armenian-Azeri conflict begun in 1988 over the sovereignty of Nagorno Karabakh.

In Eastern Slavonia and in North Ossetia/Ingushetia, the warring ethnic groups are separated by less than ten miles; we could cross from one side to the other by car, or by cars and by walking across the no-man's-land, in under an hour. Yet for several years members of these groups have not met each other face to face. Moreover through the war telephone and postal communications were severed. People are cut off from each other and the propaganda through the media and in the schools fuels the stereotyping of seeing the others as enemies. The loss of security, the economic difficulties and the feelings of humiliation, guilt and fear further fuel hate and give rise to anger and violence.

With teenagers in a school in Vladikavkaz, Roswitha was exploring the meaning of a culture of peace. When she asked about the need to live alongside other ethnic groups like the neighbouring Ingush, a deadly silence fell over the group. Nobody had dared to say the word Ingush in the school for some time. The myth of some terrible creatures seemed to hang in the air.

Roswitha had worked with some older students in that same school for about three years on personal and interpersonal issues of conflict and peacebuilding. One said "I don't know why our parents fought this war, but I don't feel any hostility towards the Ingush". It was autumn and after an English lesson with autumn leaves they collected the leaves and gave them to her as a gesture of friendship. Roswitha said she would be in Ingushetia the next day and would like to give these leaves to the students there. The Ossetian students looked at her with excitement and took the leaves and wrote messages of friendship on them.

The next day Roswitha gave those leaves to the Ingush students and told them that they came with greetings from the students in Vladikavkaz. They took the leaves, looked at them and dropped their heads. A heavy silence fell over the class. Roswitha was anxious. Gradually the students looked up and asked: did they really say these things to us? Do they remember us with friendship? When Roswitha confirmed this, the atmosphere lightened and they shared some of their good memories of living with Ossetes.

Kurtat is an Ingush village in the disputed territory. During the war it was destroyed by Russian and Ossetian artillery and incendiaries. Roswitha returned there with a former inhabitant accompanied by the special police force responsible for helping the Ingush to return to their homes. Her Ingush friend wore a thin nylon jacket on the cold autumn day. She shivered and grasping Roswitha's arm announced "I will show you the house I built". They had to get special permission to walk a further hundred yards into a field of overgrown ruins. "This was our house, I built most of it with our seven children, my husband is an invalid. Now I can't even go there and dig the ground to plant some crops".

Other displaced Ingush living there in dilapidated portacabins showed her the bullet holes on the Ossetian side of their cabins. "At night they shoot," they said, "and we are helpless." The Russian soldiers who were supposed to safeguard Ingush admitted: "We cannot do anything. You see we are here, the Ingush are on this side, and beyond are the Ossetians. If we shoot to defend the Ingush, we will hit the Ingush and not the Ossetes".

A young Ossete who really wanted to understand the Ingush better, listened to these experiences and said to Roswitha "I guess when we feel helpless we start to hate." He was trying to come to terms with the hate of his people for the Ingush.

The terrible destruction of the war between the Russian government and the Chechen forces began in December 1994. A few months later in Chechnya, Roswitha experienced people living only for the present moment. Women crouched in the temporary bazaar with goods displayed on boxes ready to grab the pile of goods and flee if the sound of gunfire came closer. People huddled outside of ruined houses swinging vodka bottles inviting her to come and see how they lived in the cellars. The driver of the taxi leaning out of the window to look for a possible ambush. The young Russian soldiers asking their Chechen enemies for bread, or salt or a cigarette. During the nightly curfew neighbours coming together to dance in the courtyard. The poignant drumbeats raising the spirits to affirm their proud Caucasian nature.

Four years later the basic utilities of water, sewerage, energy supplies have yet to be restored. The hidden costs of this war are the mounting criminality, the kidnapping, drug taking and general lawlessness arising from the lack of jobs and opportunities, and the infiltration of the fundamentalist Wahhabi sect into what was a moderate Muslim country. In this bedlam, women seek to feed and nurture their children, many of whom are severely traumatised by the violence they have seen. The invigorating spirit of holding out together against the enemy during the fighting is gone. Now that women feel they cannot even provide for their children they wonder what point there is in life.

Roswitha feels that her heart has been pierced by the pain of young Chechen boys recounting their experiences of that war, of seeing brothers shot, bodies mutilated, women tortured, and guns waved wildly by drugged soldiers. Boys that have lost fathers have now to take on the responsibility for the family. Their determination to be brave and live up to the expectations of being the oldest male in the family requires their suppression of the unprocessed pain of the war. A Caucasian can cry only three times in his life: Once when his father dies, once when his mother dies and once when his horse dies. The horse has traditionally been an essential partner in this wild mountainous region.

Roswitha is contributing to a project initiated by Dutch Interchurch Aid to help children heal their traumas by finding ways of living constructively with their experiences of war. Small groups of healing are established throughout Chechnya. Here the children feel safe, they know that in this special place they can tell their stories and cry and through games and play they can rebuild models of social interaction. These groups are facilitated by local people usually teachers. Such a group of a dozen children met in a small room in a school. The door was slightly ajar and an inspector glimpsed something of the group at work. He asked the teacher what is going on here? I have never seen anything so beautiful and tender in a school before. Parents are astonished at the effect the work has on the children, what are you doing with my daughter/son?, they ask, s/he is comple*tely changed.*

The war has left children with severe traumas caused by what they experienced or by their feelings of guilt of not preventing the death of close relatives. Not only are children haunted by nightmares and flashbacks, they also have to make leaps in their development leaving them confused. They feel that their life is disjointed from what they knew before. A part of trauma work is to restore the link with the past and to build a link into the future.

Initiatives that provide space for people to be heard, to make sense of the present, but also to vent anger, to feel dignity restored are desperately needed. The Chechen women working with children who had come to a small town in southern Russia for their training needed time and space to experience themselves in a "normal" environment. In Chechnya we have no examples of normal life, we don't know what healthy life is any more, they said.

Chechnya is a country economically destroyed by just such a war as happened in Kosovo/Serbia in 1999. Such destruction robs people of a stable future. No money, no work, ruins around. The outer destruction is the visible sign but the hidden cost is the social and psychological destruction. The social fabric of relationships and values is destroyed, community needs are abandoned whilst individual gain is selfishly sought. This is fertile time for those with big messages. The Wahhabis are imposing Sharia (Islamic) law that is feared and is alien to local traditions. Islam in the North Caucasus has always been a very moderate form with a fine Sufi philosophy.

Victims of war may seek some means of accounting for what happened such as attributing guilt to others. The emotional and psychological reasoning of their unconscious might be: "this is unbearably painful, it was not my fault, I don't want to be guilty of causing it, someone must have done it to me, I am the victim; the other is utterly bad." The "badness" of the other is then cultivated into an enemy image which justifies further violence and gives some consolation to the victims.

Guilt is a hidden cost of war. The scars of conscience borne by all who killed or injured another, especially the soldiers who are often haunted by the horrors, nightmares and nagging questions arising from the bloody mess called war. Were they merely obeying orders?, an inner voice queries. For obedience is not blind.

A whole society may struggle with this guilt knowing consciously or unconsciously that it willed the destruction of the others. After the war many books published in Vladikavkaz sought to justify the Ossetian version of it against the background of the glorious and ancient history of the "Alan" (Ossetian) people. Five years later these books were displayed less prominently, a candid admission of overdoing the prejudice.

Burdens of conscience are also borne by the many government officials who did not do all within their powers to find alternatives to violence knowing that tensions were running high and their underlying causes were not being addressed. Before the violence such officials may be devious; afterwards their blandness may be covering up a crisis of conscience for which repentance seems impossible. They are aware that they have both a public voice, the voice of the government, and a private voice that reflects what they really believe. The tension this causes can tear people apart. Peter knew a senior Soviet official driven to an early death through a heart attack caused by such tension. "I can see what I have written, I can hear what I have said, but I do not believe it". There are many such premature deaths in the North Caucasian region.

Roswitha told an Ossetian minister of her meetings with displaced Ingush refugees in their portacabins. He was responsible for their return. She conveyed her perception of their pain of living in a no-man's land situation for over five years. No work, no money and with youngsters growing up with little alternative to becoming criminals. Asking how their return could be speeded up, the minister to her distress let loose a tirade of hostile comments giving the Ingush full blame for their suffering. Their nature was to be trouble makers, any return to the disputed territory could only be because of the generosity of Ossetes. Roswitha felt trapped by this prejudice which allowed for no rational dialogue. When she said in her limited command of Russian that she could not accept such an extreme view, the minister felt that he was being called an extremist and he became angry.

We found that people were unable to acknowledge their own guilt, they could only name the guilt of the other side. To admit your and your nation's guilt in using violence might lower your self-esteem.

In war truth is the first victim. There has been nothing like the Central American or South African Truth and Reconciliation Commission in the Caucasus or the Balkans. What sparked off the violence and who then did what to whom is known if at all in confidential state enquiries and in the memory and consciences of the peoples. Much has been written by journalists about the origin and development of the Balkan wars but the wars either side of the Caucasian mountains by their very inaccessibility and the problems of language have not been well scrutinised. Listening and recording the stories of the victims of the violence there could be cathartic. We had begun to do this with the Ingush and Ossetes but the insecurity and lawlessness springing from neighbouring Chechnya have placed all that part of the North Caucasus out of bounds to any outsiders who might record these stories. They are painful, possibly provocative to the other side, and often there is only a small part of the whole truth that they reveal. Nevertheless the attention by outsiders to stories of the truth perceived by the victims of war can having healing effects.

After the Second World War people had dreams, visions, hopes for a better future. They had something to work for, their energies had common outlets. People in post-Soviet countries are utterly humiliated and in their desperate economic situation they have no image of a common future. The communist ideology of a brotherhood of nations with stern punishment for anyone fermenting ethnic unrest held people together—"in a common concentration camp",—as an Ingush official told us. Now the ideology has gone, the gates of the concentration camp are open and the people are left to fight for themselves.

During the war between Armenians and Azeris over the sovereignty of the beautiful mountainous terrain of Nagorno Karabakh, we met people displaced on both sides by the violence and their political

leaders. We saw Azeri school children bussed to the highest point of
Baku and escorted around the graves of young martyrs, boys killed by
Armenians. We were saddened by the abuse of mourning to fuel hate
for Armenians. The dead have loud voices, they need to be respected
but not allowed to jeopardise the future. What if, we wondered, those
same children were also led around the graves of young Armenians
killed by the Azeris?

Mourning is a vital element of remembering what has been lost. The
loss of lives and livelihoods is grievous, we need to weep. We found it
helpful in war-torn regions to encourage in due time the cherishing of
common memories and of mourning together. For this was how life in
community was lived before the violence and its restoration is the goal
of reconciliation.

During the civil war in Bosnia we were told of one village in which
goodwill between neighbours of different ethnicity prevailed so long as
the violence was not too close to it. But as the fighting came closer,
panic set in and the trust that had been established over centuries was
destroyed. All but one of the ethnic groups fled. Apprehension and
anxiety are vital elements in our emotion of fear. They can enable us to
survive peril, but in times of civil unrest they can so prey upon us that
we panic.

How then can we measure the hidden costs of war? That which held
people together in multi-ethnic communities is suddenly broken and
people are driven far apart physically and more importantly
psychologically. Hostile stereotypes prevail until in the softening of
time some people, often women or young people, affirm the good in
the other side or the times when they lived peacefully as neighbours.
Women are often not so attached to their self-image as men who need
such an image for their standing in society. How can such people
come together when they are physically separated and when hostile
stereotyping is still rampant? Mediators travelling between the two
sides to convey positive affirming messages that may help to heal
broken relationships.

At the end of Operation Storm in Croatia in the Autumn of 1995, the
Serbs were driven out except from Eastern Slavonia where the United
Nations Temporary Administration there, UNTAES, prevented a
further exodus. Their mandate ended in November 1997 when the
territory became fully controlled by the Croatian government. The
Serbs had the choice of fleeing across the Danube or of assuming
Croatian citizenship. Wars can end by attrition, both sides exhaust
themselves, neither is the winner. If they end by one side winning, the

other losing, the victor trades his guilt by abusing and stereotyping the loser, the loser trades his suffering and victimisation for attention. The victors persisted in imposing Croat head teachers on the schools there although 97% of the teachers and pupils were Serb. Their Serb principals were pushed aside and the contracts of all Serb teachers were made insecure.

Peter is a member of the Balkans mitigation team of the Swedish Transnational Foundation for Peace, TFF. With its director, Jan Oberg, the team was invited in the Autumn of 1997 by UNTAES just before they left to visit these schools with the concurrence of the Croatian government. At the invitation of the local education authorities schools in Croatian parts of Eastern Slavonia were also visited.

We found unaddressed and unarticulated hurt, propagated from the Croat and Serb controlled media, that fuelled stereotypes of the other as evil. On the Croat side insistence that the Serbs started the violence, and that Serbs still did not repent for the massacre of many Croats in Vukovar in 1991 whose mass graves were then still unearthed. On the Serb side, strong feelings of humiliation and insecurity, and of being victimised by the Croats. Many Serbs felt that they had no alternative to leaving as they were being "administratively cleansed". Some were in hiding since they were on a list of war criminals drawn up by the Croats. Peter met a Serb seeking emigration to Canada who had been one of the tank commanders of the Federal Yugoslav army that systematically destroyed Vukovar block by block, day by day in 1991. He was chain smoking in a village bar and drinking heavily. The owner of the bar served as our interpreter both on the Serb and Croat sides of the ethnic divide caused by the war. Constantly in her mind was the future of her young children. She was earnestly trying to convince herself that they could have a future within the Croatian Republic but her anxieties never left her. A year later she and her family were in Serbia waiting for their papers to emigrate also to Canada. Most of the Serbs in her village have like her had to sell their homes cheaply to the Croats.

Vukovar in 1997 still lay in ruins six years after the destruction of the lives and livelihoods of most of its citizens, then roughly half Serb and half Croat, living then in a beautiful town nestling in a bend of the Danube. The surviving Croats (a lot were slaughtered) were displaced a few miles to the West, and the Serbs, by far the majority in Vukovar in 1997, included many displaced from Krajina and Western Slavonia. Separated by only a few miles with UN control barriers between, the

Serbs and Croat communities of Eastern Slavonia in 1997 were alienated from each other.

To shift the log-jam of negative emotions, the TFF team found a way after several visits of bringing together in whole day seminars young Croats and Serbs aged between 16 and 19 who through their youth were innocent of the violence. We had first to persuade the Croatian Minister of Education to give her permission and encourage her regional ministers to support the venture. "Reconciliation means forgetting, we can never forget," was her first reaction. Reconciliation does not require us to forget but may require us to forgive.

With the help of regional education ministries we interviewed the principals and teachers of senior schools in the Croat and Serb regions of Eastern Slavonia. What we heard was mostly hostile of the other side—one principal in Osijek slammed down the phone on first calling him, "I won't have anything to do with Serbs," he said.

Gradually over the course of several visits we persuaded even him to permit some of his pupils to be escorted to meet Serbs in Vukovar. He even led the bus in his car and gave a brief welcoming speech to begin the seminar. Only afterwards were we told that he had been quite severely wounded during the civil war and so this first crossing after seven years into enemy territory required of him a great effort of will.

Some pupils were willing to travel to the other side to meet their peers there. We sought and generally obtained parental approval. However some mothers could not agree to their daughters engaging in this exercise: their husbands/fathers had been killed during the war. There were also some macho lads in a technical school who said that if any Serbs came to their town they would kill them. How to raise awareness amongst such lads so that they are not tempted to use violence is a challenge to us all. Fortunately UNTAES was able to disarm the population unlike the North Caucasus where there is a long tradition of keeping arms.

To begin the seminars we encouraged the Croat and Serb students to find common ground in their youth culture. Then each participant was given an opportunity to share their stories of what happened to them and their families during the war through a creative listening session in which only the person holding a Buddhist bell of mindfulness had the right to speak. In separate meetings beforehand we encouraged each ethnic group to speak only from their own experience, to use "I" statements, and not to use blaming language. Some Croat and Serb youth chose to remember the pain of violence through visiting graveyards and by planting trees of remembrance.

Croatia is a recent member of the Council of Europe and through its human rights programme some pressure was brought to bear on the Croatian government to prove that in some ways it complied with its purposes. We were invited on several occasions to comment on the proposed human rights curriculum for Croatian schools. Whilst this included many good points, it contained parts that were severely critical of its Serb minority—poems depicted Serbs as inhumane monsters. The teachers' guide made no other mention of the brutal and bloody civil war between Serbs and Croats: if it had not been for the intervention of the UN in 1995 all Serbs would have been driven out of Croatia.

Roswitha was in Moscow in May 1999 when NATO was bombing Serbia during the Kosovo war. The Chinese Embassy in Belgrade had been hit. Outside the US embassy in Moscow Chinese students demonstrated. They looked fierce and unapproachable to Roswitha and her Russian psychologist friend as they unloaded their anger and pent up emotions (arising from another hurt) on to a cause that seemed to justify all this feeling. Roswitha thought of Germans humiliated and angry when Hitler provided the match that lit the destructive fire that raged out of control.

Humiliation and hurt fan flames of violence. No emotion may be more powerful than the need to restore a sense of dignity.

Some young men from different ethnic regions of the North Caucasus told Roswitha "If we forgive, we cannot feel angry, we feel weak, it makes us feel powerless." The path to repentance, forgiveness and reconciliation is long and time consuming. It requires a transformation of perception and habits of thought. How can young men filled with the energy of anger and tempted by the sweetness of revenge be led to this path?

This article was written before the Russian offensive against Chechnya in September 1999.

A BLOODFEST

John Pilger

There were many peaceloving British people who reluctantly supported the NATO bombing of Serbia. Their views were based on the apparently very full media reports in the preceding weeks. But John Pilger's account of the self-censorship of the media after one episode of the Gulf War (written in 1991, and published in the section "Mythmakers of the Gulf War" of his book _Distant Voices_[1]) reminds us that truth is one of the casualties of war.

What ought to have been the main news event of the past week was that as many as 200,000 Iraqis may have been killed in the war in the Gulf, compared with an estimated 2,000 killed in Kuwait and 131 Allied dead. The war was a one-sided bloodfest, won at a distance with the power of money and superior technology pitted against a small Third World nation.

Moreover, it now appears that a large number of the Iraqi dead were slaughtered—and the word is precisely meant—during the brief land war launched by Washington after Iraq had agreed in Moscow to an unconditional withdrawal from Kuwait. And most of these were in retreat, ordered to withdraw, trying to get home. They were, as Colin Hughes wrote in the _Independent,_ "shot in the back".[2]

So "ring your churchbells" and "rejoice" in such a "great victory": a military operation of "almost aesthetic beauty" . . .and so on, and on, _ad nauseam._

"The glee", wrote Colin Hughes, "with which American pilots returning to their carriers spoke of the 'duck shoot' presented by columns of Iraqis retreating from Kuwait City [has] troubled many humanitarians who otherwise supported the Allied objectives. Naturally, it is sickening to witness a routed army being shot in the back." This "duck shoot", suggested Hughes, "risked staining the Allied clean-fighting war record". But no; it seems the Iraqis were to blame for being shot in the back; an Oxford don, Professor Adam Roberts, told the paper that the Allies "were well within the rules of international conduct".[3]

The *Independent* reported the deaths of tens of thousands of Iraqis on its front page, while inside a leading article referred to "miraculously light casualties"[4].

Yet the *Independent* was the only British newspaper to give consistent, substantial coverage to this slaughter. "The retreating forces huddling on the Basra beachhead", reported Karl Waldron, "were under permanent attack yesterday from the air. Iranian pilots, patrolling their border 10 miles away, described the rout as a 'rat shoot', with roaming Allied jets strafing both banks."[5] Waldron described the scene as "Iraq's Dunkirk". The Iraqi casualty figures are critical to the "great victory". Leave them out and the Murdoch comic version applies: Western technology, and Western heroism, has triumphed. Put them in and the picture bleeds and darkens; and questions are raised, or ought to be, about the "civilised values" for which "we" fought. The *Guardian* announced the death of 150,000 Iraqis in the body of a piece on page three. The *Times* and *Telegraph* performed a similar burial.[6] The next day, the *Telegraph* referred to a "massacre" on the road to Basra. American pilots were said to have likened their attack on the convoy to "shooting fish in a barrel". Ducks, rats and now fish were massacred. No blame was apportioned.[7]

On the contrary, most newspapers carried prominently a photograph of a US Army medic attending a wounded Iraqi soldier. Here was the supreme image of tenderness and magnanimity, a "lifeline" as the *Mirror* called it: the antithesis of what had actually happened.[8] Such a consensus was, to my knowledge, interrupted only once.

During a discussion about the rehabilitation of wounded soldiers, the BBC's Radio Four delivered a remarkable live report from Stephen Sackur on the road to Basra. Clearly moved and perhaps angered by what he had seen, this one reporter did as few have done or been allowed to do. He dropped the "we" and "them". He separated ordinary Iraqis from the tyrant oppressing them. He converted the ducks, rats and fish into human beings. The incinerated figures had been trying to get home, he said. Among them were civilians, including contract workers from the Indian subcontinent; he saw the labels on their suitcases.[9]

However, on the evening television news bulletins there was no Stephen Sackur. Kate Adie described the "evidence of the horrible confusion" that was both "devastating" and "pathetic". The camera panned across the "loot"—toys, bottles of perfume, hair curlers: pathetic indeed—strewn among the blackened dead. There had first been a "battle", we were told. Battle? A US Marine lieutenant looked distressed. They had no air cover, he said: nothing with which to defend themselves. "It was not very professional at all," he said, ambiguously; and he was not asked to clarify that.[10]

Apart from his words, I could find none, written or spoken, that expressed clearly the nature of this crime, this mass murder that was there for all eyes to see, and without the Iraqi Ministry of Information to "supervise" those eyes. One recalls the interrogation by satellite that the BBC's man in Baghdad, Jeremy Bowen, had to endure following his harrowing and personally courageous report of the bombing of the air-raid bunker in which hundreds of women and children died. "Are you absolutely *certain* it wasn't a military bunker?" he was asked—or words to that effect.[11] No such interrogation inconvenienced his colleagues on the road to Basra. The question, "Are you *absolutely certain* that Allied planes did *this deliberately to people running away?*" was never put.

One story never published in the British press was reported recently in the *International Herald Tribune*. It said that "estimates of the accuracy of US bombs dropped on military targets in Iraq and Kuwait suggest that hundreds of precision-guided munitions as well as thousands of 'dumb bombs' have missed their targets and in some cases struck unintended sites, according to US officials." The report described these "dumb bombs" as "simple shell-encased explosives, including some with designs dating back to World War II that follow unguided trajectories to their targets, usually hitting within 50 to 100 feet but sometimes missing by much greater distances." "Dumb bombs" were used against targets in populated areas.[12]

Perhaps the most important element in the new Big Lie concerns sanctions—the preferred alternative to killing tens of thousands of Iraqis. In a new study, the Glasgow University Media Group has found that "ironically, as the war drew nearer, evidence of the power of sanctions was just beginning to emerge", but at the same time the option of sanctions as an alternative "effectively disappeared as a news story."[13]

During this critical period, found the researchers, clear evidence was available that the effect of sanctions was "devastating"; but only the *Guardian* and the *Morning Star* argued against force; the *Guardian* quoted a CIA report that sanctions had stopped 97% of Iraqi exports. The rest of the press associated sanctions with appeasement ("Spineless appeasers"—the *Sun*). Television news contributed: "All efforts to find a peaceful solution to the Gulf crisis seemed to have ended in failure tonight" (BBC, January 15) and "War in the Gulf looks unavoidable..." (ITN).[14]

Thus, self-censorship remains the most virulent form. At the time of writing, the message of a war with "miraculously light casualties" drones on and on. There is a radio report of the trauma suffered by British troops who had to bury the victims of the atrocity on the Basra road. In the commentary, there is no recognition of the victims' human rights even in death; and no acknowledgement of the trauma awaiting tens thousands of Iraqi families for whom there will be no proper process of grief, not even a dog-tag.

Like the bulldozers that cleared the evidence on the Basra road, the propagandists here now attempt to clear away the debris of our memories. They hope that glimpses we had of the human consequences of the greatest aerial bombardment in history (a record announced with obvious pride) will not form the basis for a retrospective of the criminal nature of the relentless assault on populated areas as part of the application of criminal solutions to political problems. These must be struck from the record, in the manner of modern Stalinism, or blurred in our consciences, or immersed in celebration and justification.

Celebration, of course, is a relatively simple affair. For those of us lacking church bells, David Dimbleby will have to do. However, justification is quite another matter, especially for those who seem incessantly to describe themselves as "liberals", as if they are well aware that their uncertainty, selectivity and hypocrisy on humanitarian matters is showing. Bereft of reasoned argument, they fall back on labels, such as "far left", to describe those with humanitarian concern.

According to Simon Hoggart of the *Observer*, one of the myths spread by this "far left" is that "the Allies were unnecessarily brutal to the Iraqi forces... Of course the death of thousands of innocent conscripts is unspeakable. But you cannot fight half a war." The basis for Hoggart's approval of the "unspeakable" is apparently that his sisters are married to soldiers who went to the Gulf, where they would have been killed had not retreating Iraqi soldiers been shot in the back and Iraqi women and children obliterated by carpetbombing.[15]

Robert Harris, the *Sunday Times* man, is even more defensive. He writes that Rupert Murdoch did not tell him to support the war: a familiar refrain. Murdoch, of course, didn't have to. But Harris adds another dimension. Disgracefully, he insults Bobby Muller, the former decorated US Marine who lost the use of his legs in Vietnam, as a "cripple" and a "cardboard figure" whom I "manipulate".[16]

Even Muller, who is a strong personality, was shocked by this; and at a large meeting in central London last Monday night invoked Harris's name in the appropriate manner. Unlike Harris, he has fought and suffered both in war and for his convictions. Harris's main complaint, it seems, is that those against the war have neglected to mention Saddam Hussein's atrocities in Kuwait—which apparently justify slaughtering tens of thousands of Iraqi conscripts and civilians.

The intellectual and moral bankruptcy of this is clear. First, as children we are told that two wrongs do not make a right. Second, those actively opposed to the war are the same people who have tried to alert the world to Saddam Hussein's crimes. In 1988, 30 MPs signed Ann Clwyd's motion condemning Saddam Hussein's gassing of 5,000 Iraqi Kurds. All but one of these MPs have been steadfastly against the war. In contrast, those who have prosecuted and promoted the war include those who *supported* Saddam Hussein, who armed and sustained him and sought to cover up the gravity of his crimes. I recommend the current newspaper advertisement for Amnesty International, which describes the moving plea of an Iraqi Kurdish leader to Thatcher following Saddam Hussein's gassing of the Kurds.[17] "One of our few remaining hopes", he wrote, "is that democrats and those who cherish values of justice, peace and freedom will voice their concern for the plight of the Kurds. That is why I am making this direct appeal to you . . ." The letter was dated September 16, 1988. There was no reply. On October 5, the Thatcher Government gave Iraq more than £340 million in export credits.

1   John Pilger: *Distant Voices* (Vintage, revised edition 1994). Three paragraphs are taken from another section, "Liberal Triumphalism", in the same book.
2   The *Independent*, 28.2.1991
3   *ibid.*   4   *ibid.*   5   *ibid.*
6   The *Guardian, Times* and *Daily Telegraph*, 1.3.1991
7   The *Daily Telegraph*, 2.3.1991
8   The *Daily Mirror* 2.3.1991
9   BBC Radio 4, FM, 'Gulf Reports' frequency, 1.3.1991
10 BBC Television News, 1.3.1991
11 Jeremy Bowen was questioned by Peter Sissons on BBC Television News on 14.2.1991
12 The *International Herald Tribune*, 23-24.2.1999   [It has since emerged that some of these bombs were made of depleted uranium, whose radiation has damaged the health of Allied service personnel and Iranians, particularly children. ITV *Tonight* 26.8.99   *Editor*]
13 Greg Philo, Frank Masson, Greg McLaughlin: *Into the Media War* (Glasgow University Media Group) March 1991

14 BBC and Independent Television News, 15.1.1999
15 The *Observer*, 3.3.1991
16 The *Sunday Times*, 3.3.1991.   Robert Harris subsequently wrote to me, enclosing what he described as "a letter of apology" to Bobby Muller. Muller found no apology; Harris merely regretted not using his words differently.
17 The *Guardian*, 21.2.1991

INTERNATIONAL PEACE INSTITUTIONS

Kevin Clements

The United Nations is the main instrument of the international community for countering repression and war. A huge amount is expected of it, but it is understaffed and underfunded. Its failures are remembered, its successes often overlooked. Kevin Clements, Secretary General of International Alert, assesses it and explains what must be done to make it effective.

An Agenda for Peace

With the dissolution of the Soviet Union and the ending of Apartheid in South Africa, the world seemed poised for a period of sustained peace. The United Nations (UN) and other regional organisations were seen by diplomats and others as key actors in the evolution of the new international order. It was hoped that the end of the Cold War might mean that member states of the United Nations could settle their differences by peaceful means without the threat or use of force; or if they failed to do so it was hoped that the United Nations—without the bi-polar paralysis of the past—could take swift and resolute action to deal with acts of aggression and threats to the peace.

It was Boutros Boutros-Ghali who set about establishing a more pro-active role for the United Nations. In *An Agenda for Peace,* he mapped out four aims which have by and large defined international discussions on these topics since the mid 1990s. These aims were :

> to seek to identify at the earliest possible stage situations that could produce conflict, and to try through *diplomacy* to remove the sources of danger before violence erupts;
> where conflict erupts, to engage in *peace-making* aimed at resolving the issues which have led to conflict;
> through *peace-keeping*, to work to preserve peace, however fragile, where fighting has been halted and to assist in implementing agreements achieved by the peace-makers;
> to stand ready to assist in *peace-building* in its differing contexts:

rebuilding the institutions and infrastructures of nations torn by civil war and strife; and building bonds of peaceful mutual benefit among nations formerly at war;

and, in the largest sense, to address the deepest causes of conflict: economic despair, social injustice and political oppression.[1]

Boutros-Ghali also proposed *peace enforcement* units which could "take military action to maintain or restore international peace or security. They would be specially trained, more heavily armed than peace-keeping forces, and permanently available on call from member states. They would serve, as a means of deterring breaches of the peace, since a potential aggressor would know that the [Security] Council had some coercive capability at its disposal—thereby generating an internationally legitimate deterrent to aggression."[2]

Boutros-Ghali was obliged eventually to withdraw this suggestion as it was construed as too challenging to narrow conceptions of national sovereignty. But as Philip Wilkinson's chapter shows, the experience of the UN in Bosnia has given the idea a new relevance. It is probable that the Secretary General and the Security Council will always have difficulty deploying preventive missions or applying some measured and controlled use of force (under multilateral auspices) until the United Nations has some permanent standby forces available to it.

Even though the member states could not rise to the idea of a permanent standing force available to the Secretary General and the Security Council, *An Agenda for Peace* did revitalise the role of the United Nations in relation to pre and post conflict peace-building, peace-making, peace-keeping and peace enforcement.

The mid 1990s for example, saw much greater use of the provisions of Chapter Six of the UN Charter, legitimising peacekeeping forces (lightly armed troops from countries not involved in a specific conflict who, at the invitation of the combatant nations, would monitor cease-fires and demilitarised zones or engage in what became known as *extended peacekeeping operations*) and a more pro-active role for the Department of Peacekeeping Operations, the Department of Political Affairs and the Security Council. Chapter Seven provisions were also invoked on a number of occasions; these permitted the UN (in effect, the five permanent members of its Security Council) to enforce peace by coercive means if necessary when there was evidence of a clear threat to international peace. But the UN remained unable to deliver comfort to oppressed minority groups within countries and the citizens of repressive regimes, because of a vigorous assertion (by some of the worst perpetrators of human rights violations) of the principle of non-interference in the domestic affairs of other nations.

Yet, according to the United Nations Development Programme, as many as 90 per cent of war causalities are civilians.[3] Furthermore, internal conflicts have created the greatest forced movements of people since 1945. In 1993, there were 18.2 million refugees and 24 million internally displaced people, according to the UN High Commissioner for Refugees. By October 1994 these figures had increased to 23 million and 26 million respectively. Some estimates suggest that by the year 2000, the total could reach 100 million people.

As the 1990s draw to a close, the United Nations and many regional organisations remain as confused about their role in relation to the maintenance of International Peace and Security as they did during the Cold War. There is a lack of clarity about which UN departments have specific responsibility for peace initiatives, and how to incorporate its specialised agencies into the development of integrated responses to specific problems. There is also anxiety about the glacially slow response rate of the United Nations, particularly in relation to the prevention of gross violations of human rights or—as in the case of Rwanda—genocide. This slowness of response or worse, no response at all, has heightened popular disillusionment with the ability of the United Nations to prevent some of the most appalling slaughter of the 20th century. Richard Gott of *The Guardian,* for example, wrote:

> Overstretched and underfunded, bureaucratically and unimaginatively organised, the UN is perceived to straddle the globe like a dinosaur, fed only by the pious hopes of those (now rather elderly) people who once dreamed that it could be used to forge a better world; and by those time-serving diplomats created in each other's image who make up what is sometimes almost laughingly referred to as *the international community.*[4]

The UN is indeed rather bureaucratic and under-resourced (though most of the responsibility for that lies with the nations who fall behind with their obligatory payments and refuse to underwrite new UN peace missions). There has also been too much emphasis placed on *peacekeeping* initiatives, instead of carefully calibrated and graduated responses so that all non-violent pro-active and pre-emptive strategies can be exhausted before Chapter Six or Chapter Seven provisions are invoked. There have been far too many ad hoc decisions which do not add up to a coherent or systematic strategy for dealing with emergent conflicts all over the world. As Hugh Miall, Oliver Ramsbotham and

Tom Woodhouse write in relation to an "over-use" of peacekeeping
provisions, (especially where there is no peace to keep),

> UN peacekeeping unexpectedly became central to the response of
> the international community to an array of international-social
> conflicts, taking on unfamiliar roles in prevention (in Macedonia),
> and intervention in active war zones (in Bosnia and Somalia), as
> well as in post-settlement peacebuilding (in El Salvador,
> Cambodia and Mozambique).[5]

One of the reasons why these problems afflict the United Nations is the
generality of *An Agenda for Peace*. While it provides a helpful framework for thinking about ways of preventing and dealing with violent
conflict it does not necessarily help UN or national policy makers deal
with the specific day to day aspects of transforming an emerging
conflict; or developing an integrated UN sponsored operation in
response to complex humanitarian emergencies. In the absence of well
developed analytical and operational frameworks, desk officers cannot
write reports that provide clear alternatives, or which utilise the available information in positive ways. Miall, Ramsbotham and
Woodhouse comment:

> The difficulty of intervening in ongoing wars is exemplified in the
> ambivalent roles of UN peacekeepers in Bosnia and Somalia, the
> former tasked with protecting safe areas without being given the
> means to do so, the latter sucked into a factional conflict as one of
> the warring parties. As a result, in Bosnia the UN was accused of
> doing too little, in Somalia of doing too much.

Despite the relative success (in difficult circumstances) of UN operations in El Salvador, Cambodia, Mozambique and Macedonia, there is
no doubt that Somalia and Bosnia did enormous damage to the UN's
operational reputation; particularly for those governments who sent or
might send soldiers to future peacekeeping missions. They also severely
damaged morale within the organisation.

The UN Department of Political Affairs (DPA) is charged with analysis and policy recommendations to the Secretary General and the
Security Council; it is critical in determining whether or not peace-
making/peacekeeping operations are likely to be successful. Its success
depends on sound analysis and the mobilisation of political will (both
internal and external) to respond positively to their recommendations.
I visited the Department in 1995 to explore whether the Institute for
Conflict Analysis and Resolution, George Mason University, where I
worked, might be able to assist the DPA in these tasks.

The Department consists of extremely talented and highly experienced professionals, most of whom are completely over-stretched through lack of time and resources to carry out the tasks that have been assigned to them. The DPA only has seventy professionals working on preventive diplomacy and peacemaking. They are unable to do their job effectively because they are so pushed for time that they often cannot distinguish important from unimportant factors in emergent crises. This is because the crises they are dealing with are both more complex and have increased at a geometric rate since 1992, while the number of professional officers has not increased commensurately.

One of the clearest issues that emerged from our discussions was the inability of the DPA to learn from its own successes and failures because there is little or no time for quiet post hoc evaluations of UN interventions. This means that lessons learned in one sphere of activity cannot be applied to or tested out in other cases. There is no time for Chiefs of Mission, for example, to engage in reflective debriefing after UN operations. Although there is a "Lessons Learned" unit in the Department of Peace Keeping Operations there is no such unit in the DPA. There is a need to develop mechanisms for evaluating each UN mission in a systematic and comparative manner. This sort of debriefing could benefit from some outside facilitation by analysts (to avoid the understandable defensiveness that internal evaluations sometimes engender). The analysts could ensure that the evaluations went beyond descriptive historical narratives.

It might be useful, for example, for those who were involved in the successful ONUSAL operation in El Salvador to provide comparisons and evaluations for other operations such as Mozambique. Thus learnings could be transferred between different cases. Diplomats and UN officials need to share existing knowledge about the practical techniques that have been used in some of today's bloody conflicts. It is particularly important that the UN acquires an institutional memory about what went right and wrong in different operations. There is a need for a series of studies that might identify standard operating procedures and creative options in different types of conflict.

One possible approach might be to organise some exchanges between decision makers and academics from the field, "brain-storming" the basic approaches to conflict management, de-escalation, trust development, conflict resolution, and war termination. The most important issue might be to determine how the DPA can become more proactive, thereby closing the gap between perception of impending problems and the activation of suitable responses. There is a need to examine how complementary unofficial initiatives might assist the DPA in resolving intractable conflicts. These complementary strategies sometimes referred to as second track diplomacy—such as the eight months of secret discussions between Israelis and Palestinians in Oslo in 1992-3 or President Jimmy Carter's visit to Pyongyang in June 1994—are often able to generate responses to conflicts that elude more official negotiators.

Prevention, tracking and analysis

Whether one is counting the UN's operational costs, or the huge burden of human suffering and long-lasting instability which war causes, it is clear that prevention is definitely better than cure.[6] This is underlined in the *Report of the Secretary General on the Work of the Organisation* submitted to the General Assembly in August 1999.[7]

The UN's Department of Political Affairs, however, has difficulty exploring emerging conflicts in the absence of a specific mandate for engagement from the Security Council. Many member states feel very uneasy about the DPA taking unilateral action and "investigating" specific conflicts, or even gathering information about countries at risk. African states, in particular, are very sensitive to the notion that the United Nations might be gathering information on their internal affairs and are often wary of the intelligence gathering role of UNDP resident representatives—and even warier of envoys dispatched from New York and Geneva on "fact finding missions". Thus, although the DPA now has more flexibility than during the Cold-War era, it still has to move very cautiously.

But the DPA has to deal with some of the most intractable conflicts in the world today. The Africa Division alone, for example, has to cope with conflicts in Sierra Leone, and the Sudan, the continuing conflict between Eritrea and Ethiopia, not to mention ongoing problems within Liberia, Nigeria, Burundi, Rwanda, Angola, the Congo and elsewhere. These conflicts continue to challenge the DPA and the whole international community. There are also some important new questions about whether or not European conflicts receive more sustained attention and elicit better resourced responses than those in Africa.

There are also perennial questions about which "stakeholders" should or should not be included in pre-emptive discussions. This is particularly problematic in the case of a range of Non-State Actors who challenge official actors both politically and militarily. What is clear is that there is a need to utilise a broader range of resources than those available to the Department of Political Affairs alone.

Just as there is a need for more "joined up government" within particular countries in order that complex problems can be responded to by a range of relevant departments, so too at the international level it is important that as many relevant resources as possible are incorporated into the analysis, diagnosis and design of policy responses to situations of potential or actual violence. The insights and activities of a range of relevant national and international Non-Governmental Organisations (NGOs) should be elicited. This is particularly relevant to mapping and developing research reports on emerging threats or early warning of potential conflicts.

There are a number of organisations which currently map potential conflicts and track their development, including International Alert, the Initiative on Conflict Resolution and Ethnicity (INCORE), and the International Conflict Initiatives Clearinghouse—and others which focus on specific conflicts. Some of the information they gather can be read on the internet. Other NGOs, such as Amnesty International, Helsinki Watch, Human Rights Watch and the Minority Rights Group, act as analysts and advocates for the likely victims of oppressive regimes. Through their research and connections, they can sometimes offer contacts with key stakeholders in a potential or emerging conflict (especially non-official parties) which are unavailable to nation states or inter-governmental organisations. NGOs and academics for example can develop sound analyses of the origins and dynamics of different conflicts while second track conflict resolution practitioners might be able to design appropriate responses that will not alarm national leaders by raising the spectre of UN interference in their domestic affairs.

But more sophisticated early warning is useless without sufficient resources to "think and act in time". The policy analysts ought to know what sorts of factors should trigger serious concern—which is beginning to happen, with more co-ordination between the Secretary General and the heads of the diverse UN Departments.

It is possible, for example, to identify a range of preventive actions that can and should be exhausted before the problem is transferred to the Security Council. It is impossible, normally, to predict exactly when a tense situation will break into violence, but effective prevention does not depend on this knowledge. It depends on an awareness of the diverse ways in which tension can be reduced, and a willingness to respond to a range of early warning signals. The lack of effective early response does not normally flow from ignorance, as Judith Large points out elsewhere in this book, but from a reluctance to take early and decisive political and economic action in response to the signs of tension.

Till now there has been a lack of professional diplomatic or political personalities able to commit themselves on a long-term basis for the job of undertaking "good offices" missions. A second constraint is the lack of capital to support preventive diplomatic missions; the UN has found it difficult to get governments to finance missions before violence has broken out. These practical constraints, which are surmountable, are accompanied by political obstacles which, because, they are issues of principle, may not be so easy to overcome. The most potent of these is the fact that for the UN to act preventively it still requires the consent of at least one of the parties to the potential conflict. This is particularly salient in internal conflicts, where a government which may be involved in a counter-insurgency campaign, does not wish to internationalise the problem (like Russia over Chechnya). Often governments will resist the attentions of the Security Council as a threatening intruder which represents the interests of major powers. The other key obstacle to preventive diplomacy concerns the willingness of parties to negotiate. The need to create appropriate political will is a major feature of any design to prevent conflict. It is for these reasons that non-state actors such as NGOs may be far better equipped in such situations, and the relative advantages of NGO preventive action can be used to overcome these obstacles related to issues of state consent and sensitivities regarding sovereignty.

This issue of early warning and early responses to conflict (while they remain relatively tractable) remains one of the big conundrums on the UN agenda and it deserves more attention.

Intervention processes—from preventive diplomacy and conflict management to peace-making, peace-keeping and peace enforcement

Early warning and early response mechanisms fit most neatly with what is known as "preventive diplomacy" or pre-conflict peacebuilding. These processes are aimed at removal of the structural sources of violence and the specific precipitants which might stimulate violence. These techniques should be applied and exhausted before a conflict crosses the threshold into armed hostility.

Once conflicts have become violent, however, there is a need to think more systematically about how to restore the peace. Peacemaking has to do with all the diverse methods that are used to restore and to keep the peace after hostilities have occurred. It is to be distinguished from the peace enforcement provisions in Chapter Seven of the UN Charter in response to cross border aggression or in support of peace keeping operations.

One of the problems developing a coherent UN peace strategy has been the conceptual confusion around these diverse terms. It is not possible, for example, for peace-keepers to do their job effectively unless or until there is a peace to keep. Similarly peace enforcement operations in response to a case of cross border aggression or in support of complex peace keeping operations rarely generate the right conditions for creating long term sustainable peace. Stable peaceful relationships require much more patient identification of all relevant stakeholders, more exhaustive pre-negotiations and the development of more complex negotiating processes aimed at satisfying the needs and interests of all protagonists than is possible in a rapid Chapter 7 intervention.

The application of Article 33 provisions of the UN Charter—negotiation, enquiry, mediation, conciliation, arbitration, judicial settlement, resort to regional agencies or agreements—can be applied both before and after hostilities have taken place.[8]

For those of us with a non-violent persuasion, however, there are some additional rather onerous questions that have to be considered. In the first place we have to establish that our non-violent tools are capable of preventing violence, and/or dealing with manifest violence particularly genocide or genocidal acts of violence. If we cannot establish an ability to prevent or manage such violence then reluctantly and regretfully we might have to acknowledge the limits of non-violence and consider the application of more coercive measures such as sanctions and the limited use of military force in order to prevent avoidable suffering and death.

If the application of limited force under strict multilateral controls is to be legitimate, however, there should be an exhaustion of all non-violent negotiated solutions, a broadly based legitimation of the proposed action and well defined intervention and exit strategies. In terms of international law such force can only be authorised by the United Nations. (This is why Kofi Annan expressed such exasperation with the lack of a UN mandate authorising military action in Kosovo; strictly speaking in International Law the NATO action was only legitimate by default).

What is also clear, however, is that UN mandates for deployment would definitely be easier and faster if the Secretary General had a standing force at his or her immediate disposal. This would enable a calm appraisal of the problem, agreement on mandates and a rapid deployment of troops. Gaining the consent of state parties, mobilising the forces, agreeing command structures and operating procedures all take time. If states are reluctant to have such forces permanently deployed in strategic staging posts then it is important that a certain number of state parties have combat-ready troops available for rapid deployment under the authorisation of the Secretary General and the Security Council.

The arguments in favour of both of these strategies are obvious. They are an assertion of the primacy of the United Nations in relation to international peace and security, an ability to implement globally agreed norms and values, a capacity for some global deterrence and a heightened capacity to respond swiftly and effectively to potential or emergent humanitarian disasters. The logic of these arguments is that there should be a force (equivalent to the police for national legal authorities) available to the international community. This force would be capable of enforcing international laws and agreements. The Department for Peace-keeping Operations, for example, has been working on plans for a rapid deployment force and at least 21 governments have confirmed a willingness to provide troops to the Secretary General on a stand-by basis.

But it is also true that the problems encountered in Somalia and the former Yugoslavia have forced a reassessment of the role of peace-enforcement as a UN tool. One of the major problems which the UN Force faced in Somalia, for example, was the failure of command and control. American pre-eminence in directing the military dimension of UNOSOM II (United Nations Operation in Somalia) led to confusion and a very one-sided interpretation of the UN mandate in Somalia. The political misjudgements of American decision-makers were transformed into UN failures on the ground. In his 1993 Report to the General Assembly, the Secretary-General wrote that in UNOSOM II the "Security Council had chosen to set up an unprecedented operation involving, as necessary, enforcement action by the United Nations itself under the authority of the Security Council". There was at this time a feeling that UNOSOM II would become a model for future peace-support operations where peace-keeping functions would be accompanied by options to use enforcement measures. The decision to withdraw the UN's military mission from Somalia in March 1995, while much of the internal conflict was still continuing, reflected the need to reassess the feasibility of such an approach.

The argument against such use of force is both military and political. The military objections flow from an unwillingness to cede national military control to international institutions; a scepticism about the ability of the United Nations to determine clear and plausible goals for its military operations, concern about who would provide the resources for effective military operations and uncertainty about the effectiveness of a United Nations military command structure under the Security Council. In his *Supplement to An Agenda for Peace*, for example, Dr Boutros-Ghali indicated that at present neither the Security Council nor the Secretary-General possesses "the capacity to deploy, direct, command and control operations for this purpose, except perhaps on a very limited scale". These are important military caveats which have been reflected in some of the political objections as well. Most of these have to do with the primacy of state parties within the UN framework and anxiety about expanding and enhancing the peace and security roles of multilateral institutions. Many nation states have greater confidence in regional organisations—such as the European Union / NATO / the Association of South East Asian Nations—and a corresponding willingness to allow such organisations to develop peace and security mechanisms for dealing with violent conflict in their own regional sphere of operations. (See the arguments below in favour of enhancing the role of regional organisations in the generation of global peace and stability).

Irrespective of the merits of these two arguments, however, it is clear that the United Nations might have been able to prevent genocide in Rwanda had it acted more decisively and applied a relatively small amount of military force when called upon to do so.

The UNAMIR force in Rwanda tried to protect Tutsi in areas such as Kibuye. But because the force consisted largely of ex-colonial powers, (France and Belgium), had limited rules of engagement from the United Nations and was seen as partial to the Rwandan Patriotic Front, they were forced to withdraw. When they became concentrated in Kigali they were unable to offer any real protection to Tutsi areas outside the capital or, as it transpired, even within the capital itself. When the Belgian forces unilaterally withdrew, UNAMIR's protective capacity was critically paralysed . As late as April 7 1994, for example, (one day after the eruption of civilian violence), the UNAMIR force commander General Dallaire requested the Security Council for more troops and more forceful rules of engagement. His request was rejected by the Security Council and UNAMIR was restricted to protecting the small numbers of people who were able to shelter in areas under its control. As a consequence the UN was unable to prevent one of the biggest genocides since 1945. Andrea Telentino argues:

The total cost of the crisis to the international community was $4.5 billion, mainly in the form of humanitarian aid. Preventive action might have cost $1.3 billion. The savings are particularly large in this case because the military conflict itself was very short, but its consequences were both very expensive and quite long lasting. The immediate security problems that led to the crisis could have been dealt with relatively quickly if the international community had been willing to use force at the outset of the conflict. Officials present in the country asked for troops and an active mandate to prevent the civilian violence, but were denied. Failure to take action led not only to a civilian tragedy, but to much higher costs incurred trying to cope with it.[9]

The lessons that can be drawn from the Rwandan experience are as follows: when it is clear that a crisis has moved beyond the realm of rational and non-violent discourse and there is a reasonable probability of widespread mass violence against civilians, the United Nations should be given precise mandates, clear rules of engagement and adequate resources for effective preventive deployment of "Blue Berets". These troops should then be able to interpose themselves between the diverse warring factions in order to prevent mass slaughter. (This preventive deployment has worked effectively in Macedonia since 1992). Such deployment must be accompanied by all other processes necessary to establish the conditions for stable and lasting peace in the country, sub region or region concerned.

Hopefully, the international community will generate both the will and the resources to ensure that disasters such as Rwanda do not occur in the 21st century. It can do so by trying to avoid the negative examples of Somalia, Rwanda, Chechnya, Bosnia and by building on more positive experiences, like the preventive deployment in Macedonia or the diverse instances where different Secretary Generals of the United Nations have used their good offices to solve problems before they have gone critical.[10]

Javier Perez de Cuellar, for example, used his "good offices" to establish a Central American peace process, facilitate the withdrawal of Soviet troops from Afghanistan, end the Namibian crisis and the Iran-Iraq war, and develop proposals upon which a peace plan could be adopted for resolving Cambodia's civil war. Perez de Cuellar's initiatives were supported by Security Council action. The operations in El Salvador, Cambodia and Namibia resulted in complex mandates developed to facilitate a comprehensive peace process in each case. Perez de Cuellar had no doubt about the potential effectiveness of the

Secretary General's "good offices" function . As he put it in 1988: "No one will ever know how many conflicts have been prevented or limited through contacts which have taken place in the famous glass mansion which can become fairly opaque when necessary."

Perez de Cuellar and Boutros Boutros-Ghali both had clear ideas about ways in which the concept of preventive diplomacy could be used more effectively by the Secretary General and the Security Council in order to advance confidence, early warning, preventive deployment and demilitarised zones. They wanted to make greater use of diverse agencies such as the International Court of Justice to bring warring parties together and specialised agencies capable of applying economic assistance—carrots as well as sticks They were also very preoccupied with the necessity of developing closer co-operation between the UN and regional organisations.

A comprehensive peace-building coalition

In his 1999 report to the United Nations Kofi Annan, also acknow-ledged the critical role that NGOs can play in these delicate processes. As he puts it:

> Preventive diplomacy is not restricted to officials. Private indivi-duals as well as national and international civil society organisations have played an increasingly active role in conflict prevention, man-agement and resolution. In addressing volatile situations that could lead to violent confrontation, Governments are increasingly working in partnership with civil society organisations to defuse tensions and seek creative resolutions to what are often deep seated problems. In Fiji, for example, collaborations between NGOs and government officials, aided by quiet diplomacy on the part of regional States, resulted in the promulgation of a new constitution and forestalled what many observers believed was a real possibility of violent con-flict.[11]

In fact , what Kofi Annan and others have realised is the importance of developing a multi-faceted response to the emergency in question. Such integrated operations should engage a mixture of military, police, civilian, and technical personnel to respond to the complicated demands of modern humanitarian crises. The question which emerges from these developments is, how can a comprehensive peace-building paradigm be developed?

At present there are a number of limitations on the role of the UN in advancing preventive diplomacy. These include the logistical and financial burdens imposed by existing commitments and demands. Then there is the lack of political will amongst UN member states to act to prevent or contain the growing instabilities in the international system. It becomes clear that dealing with the sheer complexity of global problems is beyond the capabilities of a single agency or organisation. Addressing these problems requires a grand coalition of forces, drawn from a variety of different sectors and aimed at preventing and resolving the tensions which lead to war. Such a coalition would include, in addition to the UN and national governments, regional organisations, popular movements and NGOs. We must learn to utilise all the diverse instruments available to the international community in order to ensure higher levels of compliance with international norms, regimes, and legal arrangements. For example, it is to be hoped that the International Criminal Court will acquire the necessary ratifications to come into force early rather that later in the 21st century. Similarly, more use should be made of the International Court of Justice in relation to a wide range of territorial and other disputes. Only by using all the diverse institutions that exist will international institutions be able to fulfil their role as key agents in the formation of a truly global community.

In recent years, NGOs and popular movements have assumed greater importance in relation to all of these diverse issues. They have played a constantly expanding role in advancing human rights, in organising and providing humanitarian assistance, in promoting adherence to humanitarian law, fostering economic and social development, and promoting peace with justice. This "Third System" constitutes the link between "we, the people" of the UN Charter and states and the intergovernmental system. Together, NGOs represent a wealth of human and material resources that can be used to great advantage in complex and often perilous areas of action and it is they who are making the demands on both the United Nations and regional institutions to take a more pro-active role in guaranteeing international peace and human security for all.

The growth of NGOs and regional organisations such as the Organisation of African Unity, the League of Arab States, the Organisation of the Islamic Conference, The Association of South-East Asian Nations (ASEAN) and the Organisation of American States (OAS) have all made their own contributions to new ways of thinking about peace building and keeping the peace.

Some of these organisations have been bolder than others in relation to conflict prevention or preventive diplomacy. The Association of South

East Asian Nations (ASEAN) and the Organisation of American States (the OAS), for example, have very strong traditions of not interfering in one another's internal affairs unless absolutely pressed to do so. The very modest initiatives that they have adopted in response to specific crises have not provided much safeguard against repressive regimes, as examples such as Chile, Guatemala, Burma and Indonesia show. The Organisation of African Unity (OAU) on the other hand has empowered its Secretary-General to undertake mediation and fact-finding missions and to send special envoys into diverse conflict zones. Its success rate is less than stellar but it has taken some key initiatives and in doing so provided a powerful supplement to the work of the UN in relation to conflict prevention. Mahmoud Sahnoun's role as OAU Special Envoy to Brazzaville-Congo, for example, produced negotiations between the parties in a neutral country, a ceasefire, disarmament of irregular forces, and an agreement for fresh elections over disputed seats.[12] In the main, however, the real potential of regional organisations in relation to preventive diplomacy and conflict prevention is yet to be realised and the UN, NGOs and INGOs need to develop some common strategies for thinking about how best to help them become more effective.

The regional organisation which has probably developed furthest in these areas is the Organisation for Security and Co-operation in Europe (OSCE). Comprised of all the governments of East and West Europe (with Canada and USA) it was formed towards the end of the Cold War. Its most significant feature is the agreement of member states that "the commitments [we have] undertaken in the field of the human dimension are matters of direct and legitimate concern to all participating states and do not belong exclusively to the internal affairs of the state concerned." Any nation may raise a concern about abuses of human or group rights in another state, and if it finds sufficient supporters, call a meeting about it. The OSCE can provide for impartial observers in situations of imminent conflict; it was the withdrawal of its monitors from Kosovo which precipitated the crisis.

Since so many of the conflicts in Europe have an ethnic dimension, the OSCE has created the post of High Commissioner on National Minorities—currently filled by a most creative Director, Max van der Stoel. He has the duty of identifying situations of potential violence and looking for ways to prevent this happening. Miall, Ramsbotham and Woodhouse give an example of his role:

> In 1993 the citizens of Narva voted by an overwhelming majority to secede from Estonia. They were almost all

Russians who had been dismayed to become what they saw as second-class citizens in their own country. The Estonian government declared that the referendum was illegal and threatened to use force if necessary to prevent the break-up of Estonia. Russian vigilante groups began to arm themselves and in Russia the President warned that he would intervene if necessary to protect the rights of Russian speakers. At a time when it appeared that this deadlock could lead to the outbreak of fighting, Max van der Stoel, the OSCE High Commissioner on National Minorities, interceded. After meeting with representatives of Narva city council and President Meri of Estonia, he suggested that the Narva council should regard the referendum as a statement of aspiration without immediate effect. At the same time he suggested to the Estonian government that they abandon their threat to use force against the city.   His suggestions were adopted, and a potential armed conflict was avoided.[13]

In this context of highlighting the different roles of national, regional and global organisations, in relation to conflict prevention, the network of civil society and non-governmental organisations has a central role to play in advancing the concept of preventive diplomacy, facilitating conflict resolution and being the focal point for a conflict prevention conflict resolution coalition.

It has this central role because the "official sphere" often lacks the will to develop the integrated strategies necessary for preventing violent conflict, for managing existing violent conflict and for ensuring that development initiatives are aimed as much at long term stability as at short term growth. The UN's record in preventive diplomacy has been mixed. In recent years the Secretary General and the UN have managed to defuse potentially violent conflicts between Iran and Afghanistan; have done useful work in helping the demobilisation of combat forces and promoted "preventive disarmament" in El Salvador and Mozambique, and have made useful contributions towards national and regional stability in other parts of the world as well. In Namibia and Guatemala the United Nations has also experimented with the development of more holistic approaches to the implementation of the peace agreements it helped broker, thereby ensuring better prospects for conflict prevention in the future.

There is a growing awareness of the central importance in all of this of developing more coherent, inclusive strategies to peacebuilding so that a rational division of labour can be agreed between all those who can contribute to creative peacemaking. There can be no lasting peace where there are large numbers of displaced persons or refugees, so the UNHCR has a critical role to play in the development of lasting agreements. Similarly, there will be no long term structural stability and peace where the economic conditions are grossly unequal, where economic growth is stagnant or negative and where corrupt political leaders divert state revenues into private pockets. This means a heightened role in long term peace building between the international financial institutions, like the World Trade Organisation, the Bank, the IMF and the UN Development Project.

If they can all start thinking about the ways in which they do or do not make a positive contribution to peaceful relationships, that too will go a long way toward ensuring that their decisions do not generate unpeaceful relationships as has happened many times in the past, in, for example, draconian structural adjustment programmes or ill founded development projects. This means that all UN institutions need to place more priority on people-centred security in conflict zones; conflict impact assessments should accompany all international economic and social development programmes[14] and there should be a sustained attention to the promotion of good governance in relation to all comprehensive peace agreements and post-conflict reconstruction packages.

The changing nature of UN activities in peace and security has brought the NGO community into closer contact with the Organisation on the ground, especially in humanitarian relief and post-conflict peace-building. This has brought the two systems of state-centred interests and civil society interests into close contact. The non-state nature of NGOs and their familiarity with the societal structures which are at risk in potential conflict situations makes them ideal for identifying tensions which are all too often precursors to societal violence. This closeness and the inevitable links which are created among the different sectors of civil society means that NGOs are very well placed to influence or facilitate processes towards dialogue. The successful experience of this form of conflict resolution has demonstrated the merits of NGO action; from the Buddhist monks and peace-marchers of Cambodia to the Catholic Bishops and civic organisations in Latin America; from the multi-sectoral peace advocates and peace-zone communities in the Philippines[15] to the community groups and NGOs involved in improving Catholic-Protestant relations in Northern Ireland,[16] and the tribal elders of Somaliland[17] who have used traditional forms of local diplomacy to resolve resource-based conflicts in the north of their country. The requirement for a successful new agenda is the employment of these methods at an early stage before violent conflict has broken out, using the relative strengths of the international community to achieve this objective.

What are the lessons of all this?

It is clear that the conflict arena is multi-layered, needing different types of preventive action. There are at least five layers, the personal, the local, the national, the regional and the international. Different actors, intervening at appropriate intervals and using relevant tools can construct a cohesive network for preventive action and conflict resolution. As this chapter has illustrated, this includes the UN and its agencies, regional organisations and NGOs.

At the heart of this design and preventive action plan is the concept of multi-track diplomacy.[18] This is the application of peacemaking from different vantage points within a multi-polar network. Neither first-track or second track diplomacy can encompass the extraordinary value of a more multi-dimensional approach. Eleven types can be identified:

(1) inter-governmental diplomacy such as the United Nations,
(2) governmental peacemaking through official diplomacy such as the bilateral negotiations between the parties in the Middle East,
(3) second track diplomacy using unofficial forums such as the secret Norwegian negotiations which eventually led to the 1993 peace deal between Israel and the Palestinian Liberation Organisation (PLO),
(4) citizen diplomacy through private means; this can come in many forms but one of the most successful illustration of this is in Somaliland where tribal elders have used traditional kinship networks to resolve conflicts,
(5) economic diplomacy includes donor assistance from a variety of donor agencies which work towards an economic package for sustaining peace,
(6) peace diplomacy through religious organisations; this not only encompasses the work of local churches and religious leaders but also projects established by international religious establishments such as the World Coucil of Churches, the Quakers or the Italian-based Catholic lay community of Sant' Egidio,
(7) diplomacy through women's movements, which both at a local and international level, has helped mobilise women in the pursuit of conflict resolution,

(8) communications diplomacy through the media has proved to be a particularly powerful tool in mobilising public opinion and moulding the perceptions of policymakers,

(9) peace diplomacy through social movements is a broader form of the citizen diplomacy described above and examples of this may include the "peace zones" and "peace corridors" created by communities in Colombia and the Philippines, or the work of the Community Relations Council (CRC) in Northern Ireland,

(10) peace education through education and training which addresses some of the root causes of conflicts; projects such as UNESCO's "Programme to Promote a Culture of Peace" and International Alert's training seminars and workshops in the Near East, Africa and Latin America are examples of this form of diplomacy,

(11) creative diplomacy through artists and personalities from the world of entertainment such as "Live Aid", "Band Aid" and "Comic Relief".

Besides using all these tracks there needs to be substantial reform within the UN, ensuring that the UN Security Council is more representative of the global polity, removing the anachronistic veto power assigned to only five nations, and strengthening the Office for Preventive Diplomacy and the High Commissioner for Human Rights. With so many conflicts centred on contending national claims it is important to create a structure within the UN system for dealing yet again with cases of self-determination. In addition an argument can be made for the revival of an International Trusteeship system. In cases of failed or failing state institutions, and where civilian lives may be at risk from competing warlords and factional warfare, a trusteeship under UN auspices may be a viable option.

Since September 1945, there has never been a day without war. On average a new war has begun every three months. By 1992 their death toll amounted to over twenty million. Yet the 279 vetoes cast in the Security Council in that period showed how the major powers, including Britain, denied it an effective peace role. The question is whether or not there is a will on the part of all member states to ensure that the United Nations, along with the diverse regional IGOs, national and global NGOs, can indeed become a centre for the effective promotion of peace, security and justice for all in the 21st century.

The first principle of the UN Charter "is to save succeeding generations from the scourge of war..." However, it is clear that intergovernmental organisations such as the UN and individual governments have not and will not be able to meet this challenge by themselves. Nor can we expect undemocratic or defective governments to address the underlying causes of violent conflict without sustained pressure from ordinary people, non-governmental organisations, social movements and others concerned with peace, justice and human rights.

So what is needed to ensure that the aspirations of the Founders will become a reality in the 21st century? In the first place it needs an explicit coalition of the willing states and non-state parties to breathe fresh life into the Charter's aspirations. Second it requires much higher levels of strategic planning and coordination between diverse humanitarian agencies, development agencies, human rights groups, humanitarian law agencies, military representatives, local and international peace groups, social movements, the media, business leaders, parliamentarians, municipal leaders, religious groups, scholars and artists. Third, it requires a determination to act decisively whenever there is warning of small or gross violations of human rights which might threaten the peace and generate violence. Fourth, we need to believe that peace is possible so that it may be realised in all that we do—economically, socially, culturally, politically and militarily. There is no better time to think about these things than at the beginning of the new millennium. We can only hope, with the Quaker pioneer in conflict studies Kenneth Boulding, that the 21st century will indeed be the century of maturity and we will all discover new and creative non-violent ways of dealing with injustice, repression, and unpeacefulness. Only by a radical commitment to this principle will we ensure that all our national, regional and global institutions will truly serve the human interest and advance human security.

1   Boutros-Ghali, B. *An Agenda for Peace* (New York: United Nations, 1992)
2   *ibid.*
3   UNDP *Human Development Report* (New York, 1994) p.47
4   Richard Gott: "Death of a Dinosaur" *New Internationalist* N° 262, December 1994
5   Hugh Miall, Oliver Ramsbotham, Tom Woodhouse: *Contemporary Conflict Resolution* (Cambridge: Polity, 1999) p. 141–2
6   See Michael E Brown and Richard N Rosecrance: *The Costs of Conflict:Prevention and Cure in the Global Arena* (Carnegie Commission on Preventing Deadly Conflict, Maryland and Oxford, Rowman and Littlefield 1999). This book establishes clearly that even though prevention is costly it is definitely cheaper in terms of human, physical and economic capital than late enforcement action. It demonstrates this with a

series of case studies of failed prevention in Bosnia, Rwanda, Somalia, Haiti and the Persian Gulf; some examples of "initial prevention" in Macedonia, Slovakia and "mid course prevention" in Cambodia and El Salvador. In each of these examples, it is clear that focussing global resources towards prevention is both cost effective and politically effective.

7   See *Report of the Secretary-General on the Work of the Organisation* , 31 August 1999 Supplement No.1 (A/54/1) especially paras 66-88 in which the SG indicates that early warning is now agreed to be a necessary condition for effective preventive diplomacy but it is unfortunately not a sufficient condition as evidenced by the tragedy in Kosovo where diplomatic efforts failed and destructive military logic prevailed. On the other hand as he notes, there have been other quiet initiatives such as the UN brokered deal between the Government of Morocco and the Frente Polisario that broke the impasse over a referendum for self determination now agreed for 31 July 2000.

8   See Gareth Evans: *Cooperating for Peace:The Global Agenda for the 1990s and Beyond* (Sydney: Allen and Unwin, 1993). He elaborates the differences between preventive diplomacy, preventive deployment, peace-making, peacekeeping, sanctions, and peace enforcement. Each one of these strategies has a role to play in the construction of stable peace but it is important that all the non-violent methods be exhausted before sanctions and force are applied, otherwise these "deterrent options" lose their capacity to deter.

9   Andrea Kathryn Talentino, "Rwanda" (in Brown and Rosecrance *op cit*) pp. 72-73.

10 M. Franck & G. Nolte, "The Good Offices Function of the UN Secretary-General" (in Adam Roberts & Benedict Kingsbury, eds: *United Nations, Divided World* (Oxford, Clarendon Press, 1993) p.144

11 Secretary General's Report for 1999, *op cit*. § 39-40

12 M. Lund: *Preventing Violent Conflicts* (Washington DC: US Institute of Peace. 1996) p. 74

13 *op.cit.* p. 99

14 International Alert, for example, in conjunction with Safer World is developing peace and conflict impact assessment methodologies in order to enable public and private aid donors to ascertain the likely consequences of their policies, programmes and projects on peaceful reationships. (For more information contact Manuela Leonhardt at International Alert, 1 Glyn Street London SE 11 5HT)

15 E.Garcia (ed) *Pilgrim Voices: Citizens as Peacemakers*, (International Alert/Manila: Atheno de Manila University Press, 1994)

16 John Lampen: *Building the Peace* (Belfast: Community Relations Council, 1995)

17 Dr A.Yusuf Farah & Prof. I M .Lewis: *Somalia: The Roots of Reconciliation*, (London: ActionAid, 1993)

18 For the most detailed exposition of this perspective see John McDonald and Louise Diamond: *Multi Track Diplomacy: A Systems Approach to Peace* (Washington DC: IMTD. 1996)

SEARCHING FOR A JUST PEACE

Elizabeth Salter

The Christmas message is "peace on earth", but for centuries the churches encouraged and sometimes themselves waged war. It is only is recent times that, challenged by the example of Christians like Martin Luther King Jr and Desmond Tutu, the main churches have embarked on an agenda of peace, defined by King as "True peace is not the absence of tension: it is the presence of justice". Elizabeth Salter describes the change.

Vancouver, 1983. The Sixth Assembly of the World Council of Churches, the body founded in 1948 to give form and content to the desire of mainstream churches throughout the world to work and pray together. Delegates to the Assembly, representing churches of many traditions, Orthodox, Protestant, Anglican, instructed the WCC to pursue a new programme priority. It was "to engage the churches in a conciliar process of mutual commitment to justice, peace and the integrity of all creation".

JPIC, as the process was soon known, picked up on emphases which were already vital to the life of the ecumenical community. For many years the struggle for justice had been the major priority of many member churches, particularly in newly independent countries, those with oppressive regimes and those with few material resources. The cry for justice was a compelling one for Christians committed to the struggle against apartheid in South Africa, to the toppling of dictators such as President Marcos of the Philippines, to the elimination of hunger in countries plagued by drought, floods or disease. The call for closer attention and care to be given to the God-given gift of creation in all its amazing diversity, was also being heard and responded to by an increasing number of people, both secular and religious. Peace, too, and the prevention of armed conflicts, had been the subject of resolutions and consultations, ever since the First Assembly of the WCC, meeting in Amsterdam in 1948, had agreed that

"War as a method of settling disputes is incompatible with the teaching and example of our Lord Jesus Christ. The part

41

which war plays in our present international life is a sin against God and a degradation of man."

There had been many attempts to commit the member churches to the promotion of peaceful resolution of conflicts, particularly during the Cold War and the nuclear arms race. The threat of the use of nuclear weapons led many to re-examine the tradition of a just war[*], which has for centuries provided guidelines for churches of several traditions. Whilst the option for pacifism and non-violence has been advocated most consistently and persistently by the Historic Peace Churches— Quaker, Brethren, Mennonite—an increasing number of mainstream churches now responded to the call of the Vancouver Assembly to take seriously the interlinking themes of justice, peace and the integrity of creation. The German physicist, Carl Friedrich von Weizsacker, called for a new ecumenical Council, following on the great councils of the early Church, devoted to peace as an essential Christian theological responsibility of the time.

The World Convocation on JPIC, held in Seoul, S. Korea, in 1990, did not go as far as many of its supporters hoped it would in bringing about such a great Council, but it did lay down some important guidelines for future work, "We are called to seek every possible means of establishing justice, achieving peace and solving conflicts by active non-violence" stated participants, calling for the rejection of systems of security based on weapons of mass destruction and military invasions, interventions and occupations. The practice of non-violence in personal relationships, and the rejection of "the spirit, logic and practice of deterrence based on weapons of mass destruction", were affirmed, as well as the development of a culture of active non-violence "which is life-producing and is not a withdrawal from situations of violence and oppression but a way to work for justice and liberation".

Such statements were music to the ears of Quakers and others in the Historic Peace Churches who had often waited in vain for a response

---

[*] Just war criteria are divided into those by which it is determined that it is just to resort to war (*jus ad bellum*): 1. There must be a just cause. 2. The aims of the war must follow a just intent, i.e. the pursuit of a just peace. 3. War must be a last resort. 4. War can be made only by legitimate authority, i.e. a sovereign government or competent international body. 5. There must be a reasonable prospect of success; and those applicable to decisions taken in midst of war (*jus in bello*): 6. War must honour the principle of discrimination, requiring noncombatant or civilian immunity, and avoiding massacres, atrocities, looting or wanton violence. 7. Violence applied in war must be restrained by the principle of proportionality.

from mainstream churches to Jesus's challenging call to be peacemakers. But would they turn out to be yet another set of fine words, lost in the welter of soon-to-be-forgotten verbiage which too often characterises the churches' solemn pronouncements? Churches have for centuries been especially skilled in the ignoble art of shooting themselves in the foot, and perpetrating conflict, either between themselves, or directed against those who either do not agree with them or who get in their way. The Wars of Religion, the Crusades, the Inquisition, the colonisation of Central and South America, the justification for slavery, and. in more recent times, the alliances between narrow nationalists and particular religious denominations, inspire little confidence in the peacemaking skills of those who profess and call themselves Christians.

On the other hand, there are remarkable examples of thoughtful attempts by members of the Christian churches to tackle violence at many different levels. Those who have taken Jesus' call to his followers to be peacemakers as an essential part of the gospel, and not just an optional extra, have shown what it means in life-threatening situations: Dietrich Bonhoeffer, the great German theologian and pastor, who was hanged by the Nazis because of his "costly discipleship"; Martin Luther King, who died a martyr's death, passionate for justice for his fellow black Americans, yet determined to seek it by nonviolent means; the Corrymeela Community and other interdenominational groups in Northern Ireland, patiently committed to peacebuilding, for decades bringing all sides in the long-standing conflict together in a safe place, for debate and discussion; churches in Los Angeles holding hearings after race riots, helping rival gangs to meet, to speak of their grievances, to decide together on strategies for community building; the Viva Rio movement in Rio de Janeiro, Brazil, sponsored by the churches to resist violence in the streets.... many positive stories of selfless, sacrificial action by groups and individuals, often unknown and unsung.

Then I joined the staff of the WCC in 1990, working within its Commission of the Churches on International Affairs, my initial task included travelling widely in Central and Eastern Europe, listening to people in the churches which were emerging from long periods of oppression into a totally new situation, trying to help them to respond to fresh challenges and discern priorities. The euphoria of those early heady days was soon replaced by problems of a different and sinister kind. Many of the resentments which had been forcibly repressed by Communist regimes began to surface. Like Pandora's box, once the lid had been lifted, there was no question of putting it tightly back into

place again. Even before the bloody battles in former Yugoslavia—
Bosnia, Croatia, Kosov@*—there were other disputes fomenting, in
Romania, in the Baltic States, in the former Soviet Union.

It had always been part of the mandate of the CCIA to seek ways of
using the influence of the churches, at local, national and international
level, to help in the search for solutions to political problems. We had,
for instance, since 1984, been building bridges between Christians in
South and North Korea, two countries divided for over forty years by
an impenetrable wall—both physical and political—yet in reality a
single nation for many centuries. A series of encounters in Japan and in
Switzerland led to some historic ecumenical visits to the tiny Christian
communities in North Korea, and to the opening of a tiny chink in the
armour of suspicion and mistrust which has typified relations between
the two Koreas for so long. The churches were in a unique position to
take those steps. They had no political axe to grind, and their desire to
reestablish human and spiritual contacts which had been so cruelly
severed were manifest to both sides. Such trust-building at a personal
and community level was intrinsic to the establishment of trust at
international level. Fifteen years further on, we can see how important
those communications were in the slow, patient process of breaking
down the walls of hatred and building new relationships.

In the ecumenical movement we had so much to do. Our assignments
were all connected to the pressing need to promote and build positive,
creative relationships between individuals, communities and nations.
One such task we took on board was in the Caucasus. Soon after the
break-up of the Soviet Union and the formation of newly independent
states, a violent conflict broke out between Armenia and Azerbaijan
over the tiny enclave of Nagorno-Karabakh. Both states claimed the
territory as their own, and the destruction of homes and livelihood was
immense, as was the movement of populations between the two
countries, with close on a million refugees on both sides.

Here was a situation, we believed, where the religious communities—
the majority Armenian Apostolic Church, one of the founder members
of the WCC and the majority Muslim community in Azerbaijan—who
were not themselves in conflict, could make a significant contribution
to bringing the war to an end. A small team of us visited the two
countries (a major undertaking in itself!), met with the political
authorities and held talks with the Armenian Catholicos (or Patriarch)
and the Azeri Sheik-ul-Islam, leader of the Muslims in the whole

---

* This nonpartizan spelling combines the Serbian version KosovO and the
Albanian version KosovA.

Caucasus region. We convinced the two men of the value of a meeting at a private venue in Switzerland. (The Sheik-ul-Islam told us: "This is something I have heen trying to do for a long time... but only you can do this for us.") The result of that 1998 meeting, after many hours of lengthy discussion between the two religious leaders and their advisers, was a joint statement, which, amongst several practical proposals, denounced war as a means of settling disputes, and called on the warring parties to settle their differences by peaceful negotiation.

The war is over now, though real trust-building will take much longer to accomplish. Nevertheless, the major religious bodies in the region were attempting what was most appropriate for them: to bring reconciliation where communities had been torn apart, and healing to their wounded nations.

January 1994 marked a major step forward in the determination of the member churches to take their peacemaking role seriously. At the WCC Central Committee meeting, held in Johannesburg, South Africa, delegates heard an impassioned sermon preached at the opening service by Methodist Bishop Stanley Mogoba. He thanked the WCC for the achievements of the Programme to Combat Racism, which had done so much in the struggle against apartheid, and to the establishment of democracy in South Africa. But the new foe, here as in so many parts of the world, was endemic violence. Could not the WCC begin a new campaign? A few days later, the delegates voted unanimously to establish a Programme to Overcome Violence, "with the purpose of challenging and transforming the global culture of violence in the direction of a culture of just peace". I seldom find cause to get emotional at ecumenical gatherings, but I confess, at that moment of decision, the tears were rolling...

I soon found myself with the job of setting up the new Programme, and busily engaged in organising consultations and publishing material to help the churches get involved. There was work to be done on the theological dimensions of the programme: although the WCC had published many documents on questions such as political ethics, and new theological approaches to issues of peace and war, there was now the stated objective of considering whether the churches should now face the challenge to "give up any theological or other justification of the use of military power, and to become a *koinonia* (fellowship) dedicated to the pursuit of a just peace". The whole Council had to be drawn into the Programme. Even those coping with situations such as the aftermath of the genocide in Rwanda, were now adding to their programmes of aid the need for conflict resolution skills. We were not just dealing with the results of failed traffic lights, and tending the wounded. We were trying to prevent the traffic lights from failing yet again.

Over the past few years the programme, led by my successor Salpy Eskidjian, has concentrated on sharing with the member churches the experience of seven major cities, one in each continent, where violence has been a major problem: Belfast, Boston, Rio de Janeiro, Suva, Colombo, Durban and Kingston (Jamaica). The "Peace to the City Campaign" included visits and information sharing, and exploring new ways of spreading the message and practice of nonviolent conflict resolution.

The conviction that violence at all levels, personal, local, national and international, has the same roots, and that overcoming it must now be a major priority for the churches, led the 1999 Central Committee to declare the first ten years of the new Millennium an "Ecumenical Decade to Overcome Violence". It invites churches to reflect and act on that theme from Christian perspectives, and will run simultaneously with an UN decade to protect children from violence.

For members of the Historic Peace Churches, these moves on the part of the mainstream churches mark an astonishing, and profoundly welcome leap forward, a twenty-first century commitment. In the words of Konrad Raiser, the WCC's General Secretary: "It is my hope and prayer that as an ecumenical community we will be able, through this decade, to render a faithful witness to the One who is our peace and who has broken down the dividing wall of hostility". The world will continue to need that commitment.

INTERNATIONAL CRIMINAL LAW AS A DETERRENT MEASURE

Bernard F. Hamilton

Bernard Hamilton is an expert in international and human rights law, and President of the Leo Kuper Foundation which tries to eliminate genocide. Here he describes how the International Criminal Court can help to prevent state repression.

The Reach of International Criminal Law

In November 1999, former Ethiopian leader Mengistu Haile Mariam visited South Africa for medical treatment. From 1974 to 1991, his regime had been in power as thousands of Ethiopians were murdered, tortured or "disappeared". Thousands more died as a result of the regime's policy of forced relocation. Mengistu had lived in neighbouring Zimbabwe since he was deposed in 1991. At the prompting of human rights groups, South Africa's Minister of Justice asked the Director of Public Prosecutions to investigate the possibility of charging Mengistu with crimes against humanity. Before a case could be brought in South Africa's court, Mengistu had slipped across the border back to Zimbabwe.[1]

A few months earlier, Ezzat Ibrahim Douri, a highly placed member of the Iraqi regime, had to cut short a visit to Vienna once his whereabouts became generally known. Vienna city councillor Peter Pilz filed a complaint with the Austrian state prosecutor for his alleged involvement in crimes against the Kurds of northern Iraq during security force actions of 1988 and 1991.[2] Those accused of violating international criminal law now know that they risk prosecution whenever they travel overseas. Mengistu is wanted for crimes against humanity in his own country Ethiopia. A change of government in Zimbabwe could result in his arrest. This is known as the Pinochet effect, because of the arrest of Chile's former head of state.

In October 1998, Augusto Pinochet was wanted on charges relating to the torture of Spanish citizens in Chile during the time he had been in charge there. Pinochet calculated that it would be safe to visit Britain, but he failed to consider Baltasar Garzon the Spanish magistrate who applied for his extradition. Pinochet spent over a year under house arrest in London as he chose to contest the extradition rather than answer the charges in Spain.

What the world is witnessing, is a change in States' attitudes towards the sovereign right of political leaders to exercise power in violation of international criminal law. At present, we are simply observing leaders changing their travel plans. It is though a short step from there to a situation where leaders reason that it makes more sense to change their behaviour. Leaders who know that a violation of international law will probably result in prosecution are likely to be deterred from embarking on such a course of action. Some leaders may be sufficiently disturbed to miscalculate and advocate a criminal solution to their perceived problems. However, their subordinates are less likely to follow them, as they reflect on the long arm of justice reaching across international borders and through the years to hold murderers and torturers to account.

Changing Attitudes to International Criminal Law

It is not clear why, at the dawn of the twenty-first century, states are starting to prevent and punish international crimes.[3] Some commentators argue that the main factors are the emergence of democracy as the dominant political system in the world, and the development of information technology which provides reliable accounts of violations around the globe almost as they occur.[4] The 1991 public reaction to scenes of Kurdish refugees in Northern Iraq is said, for example, to have prompted Western leaders to push for United Nations Security Council Resolution 688, which demanded an end to repression in Northern Iraq over a month after the liberation of Kuwait.[5] This increased readiness to enforce international criminal law is remarkable for a number of reasons. Firstly, numerous states traditionally allow their international dealings to be dominated by economic, strategic or similar considerations of "realpolitik" rather than ethical principles. Secondly, some states lack highly developed judicial systems. Put simply, such states are already over-stretched without adding international law cases to their courts' crowded dockets. Thirdly, each state's constitution will accord international law different status. One constitution, such as Austria's for example, will give treaties precedence over existing or subsequent legislation. Another constitution, such as that of the United Kingdom, requires incorporation of treaties into domestic legislation before they can take effect. Despite these differences, a growing number of states are either seeking to bring international criminals before their own courts or working together to create international tribunals that can try cases.

The Development of International Criminal Law

Although extradition provisions are recorded in treaties dating back over 3000 years, and an ad hoc international war crimes tribunal existed in 1474, it was Nuremberg that provided the real impetus to international criminal law. The Nuremberg Tribunal not only tried leaders for war crimes and crimes against peace, but also for the newly codified crimes against humanity, including genocide. It demonstrated, in a way that the World War I peace settlement had failed to do, that individuals who commit international crimes can expect to face justice. The Tribunal established that anyone committing, or complicit in, an international crime is individually answerable and liable for punishment. A state's laws cannot prevent this and there is no immunity for heads of state or government officials. The UN formally recognised these as the Nuremberg Principles in 1946,[6] and they were formulated by its International Law Commission in 1950.[7]

In establishing that such crimes as genocide, war crimes and torture were crimes against the whole of humanity, the Nuremberg Tribunal underscored the right of every state to investigate, prosecute and punish such crimes, no matter where they had taken place. This is known as the principle of universal jurisdiction. Some states have taken on an additional responsibility, the obligation to prosecute. This obligation is provided for in such treaties as the 1948 Convention on the Prevention and Punishment of the Crime of Genocide[8] and the 1984 Convention against Torture and other Cruel, Inhuman or Degrading Treatment or Punishment.[9] Further, the international community has emphasised the gravity of such crimes by adopting the 1968 Convention on the Non-Applicability of Statutory Limitations to War Crimes and Crimes against Humanity, which makes clear that there is no time limit for the prosecution of crimes against humanity or war crimes. In 1998, for example, France convicted Maurice Papon for complicity in crimes against humanity committed over fifty years previously during the Holocaust.[10]

The Post Cold War Era

Despite the growing recognition of the international community that the whole of humanity had an interest in seeing certain international crimes prosecuted, Cold War fears seemed to constrain states from exercising jurisdiction in their own courts or from creating international courts of the kind envisaged by the 1948 Convention on the Prevention and Punishment of the Crime of Genocide. Israel's prosecution of Adolph Eichmann in 1961 provided an exception to this; but as a Jewish state, Israel had a compelling interest in prosecuting the head of the Nazis' Jewish Office. During the 1990s, the UN Security Council established two international criminal tribunals to prosecute crimes committed after the Cold War in the former Yugoslavia[11] and in Rwanda.[12] Both tribunals have experienced difficulties in persuading states to deliver suspects to the court. More recent moves to find a state willing to try Cambodia's Pol Pot for crimes committed in the 1970s were not successful.[13] It appears that such states as Israel and Spain are more willing to prosecute where their link with the victim provides them with a state interest.

Despite the relative security of the post Cold War era, in which two international criminal tribunals are providing judicial interpretations of current international criminal law, states remain reluctant to exercise universal jurisdiction over an agreed code of humanity. The establishment of a world court of criminal jurisdiction would encourage states to exercise this. Such a court would be able to investigate and prosecute international crime when states proved to be unable or unwilling. The very presence of such a court would doubtless act as an incentive for those states that had a prosecutorial capacity to exercise it, since such states would not wish to be seen to fail to uphold the law. This was the great hope of many of those who supported the early establishment of the International Criminal Court—that it would provide the vital cog in the machinery of international relations that will deter the operation of repressive regimes. Such a court will soon come into existence.

Introduction to the International Criminal Court

Early in the twenty-first century, there will be a court door on which anyone may knock. Victims, their families and other interested parties from anywhere in the world will be able to approach the Court's Prosecutor in search of justice for those who have suffered as a result of genocide, crimes against humanity or war crimes. If they succeed, their story could be told, guilt officially acknowledged, the perpetrator sentenced and compensatory damages awarded. Such justice could be a step towards reconciliation and, more significantly for our present purposes, a deterrent to others.

The new International Criminal Court (ICC) will come into being after 60 states have ratified the Court's Statute.[14] The Statute was adopted by 120 states at a conference convened by the United Nations in 1998, after several years of deliberation. At December 27, 1999, six states had ratified the Statute, and 92 had signed it as an indication of their intention to ratify.

The Crimes

The ICC will cover the most serious crimes known to international law: genocide, crimes against humanity and war crimes, whether committed during international conflict or, more importantly, during internal conflict where so many atrocities have occurred in recent years. The Court will also have jurisdiction over the crime of aggression, which refers to the unprovoked attack by one state against another, once the States Parties have formulated a precise definition.

The Court

The new Court will be in the Hague, which is currently the home of the International Court of Justice and the International Criminal Tribunal for the former Yugoslavia. The Court will complement states, and not have jurisdiction where states are able and willing to exercise jurisdiction themselves. It will not have jurisdiction over crimes committed before its existence. There is no statute of limitations, which means a criminal may live in fear of prosecution until the end of their days.

The Judges

Like the other Hague courts, the ICC will have no jury. It will have 18 judges, elected for non-renewable terms of nine years by the States Parties. The Statute provides for representatives of the world's main legal systems as well as geographical balance, and competence in criminal law and relevant international law. More interestingly, the Statute requires the Court to ensure judicial expertise on relevant issues including violence against women or children. The bench must also include a fair representation of both genders among its judges, and many people will be watching to see how that is interpreted.

Admissibility

The Court may consider cases referred to it by the UN Security Council, by States Parties or by the Court's Prosecutor. It is possible

that there may not be many referrals from the Security Council
because it frequently becomes deadlocked. Similarly, although states
have taken some disputes to the International Court of Justice, none
have ever accused another of violating any of the six core human rights
treaties, and so states are not likely to forward many cases to the
Court. For this reason, the Prosecutor is likely to be the best source of
referrals. The Prosecutor may seek information from any source,
including civil society organisations, and may hold preliminary examination hearings in the Hague.

If, as a result of the preliminary examination, the Prosecutor wishes to
launch an investigation, he or she must get the consent of a three-judge
chamber. At this point, any state which is entitled to exercise jurisdiction over the crimes concerned has one month to take over the investigation. The Prosecutor must then obtain approval from the Pre-trial
Chamber to continue, or else the case is deferred to the state.
Furthermore, a state can appeal the decision of the Pre-trial Chamber.
Even if this appeal fails, the state may still prevent prosecution at the
ICC by demonstrating that it is investigating or prosecuting the case or
has done so. In addition, the UN Security Council may block an investigation or prosecution for renewable periods of one year. Such a move
would require each of the Security Council's five Permanent Members
to refrain from exercising their veto.

Reparation

A feature of the new court that owes much to the concerns of civil
society organisations is reparation. The Court may imprison convicted
criminals, normally for up to thirty years, but exceptionally for life. It
can also fine someone and confiscate any proceeds from the crime.
The Court may order fines and forfeitures to be placed in the Court's
trust fund for the benefit of victims and their families. The ICC is also
empowered to make an order against a convicted person in respect of
reparations that would include restitution, compensation and rehabilitation. Before making this order, the Court may invite representations
from the convicted person, victims and other interested persons or
states. States' Parties must assist the Court in the collection of fines
and forfeitures, including the freezing of assets for eventual forfeiture.

The Court's Promise

The ICC Statute holds considerable promise. It is not a perfect document. The Prosecutor must surmount many hurdles before he or she

can commence a trial, and the definitions of some crimes raise high thresholds. However, the Statute establishes an independent prosecutor. It has espoused some gender aspects of international justice, and other developments recognised in the jurisprudence of the Inter national Criminal Tribunals for Rwanda and for the former Yugoslavia. It offers reparation to those who have suffered. As a body of impartial, independent expert and disinterested judges drawn from the world's main legal systems, the Court's findings are certain to find broad acceptance. It is likely to provide an incentive to states to exercise jurisdiction over international crimes, and it will have the effect of deterring crimes.[15]

Conclusion

In this chapter, we have traced the growth of international criminal law through the work of the Nuremberg Tribunals of 1946, the adoption of subsequent treaties and statements of principles, the work of the two ad hoc tribunals created by the UN Security Council during the 1990s and the Statute of the International Criminal Court.

We have seen a greater willingness on the part of states to prevent and punish international crime, particularly in the post-Cold War era. We concluded that states were reluctant to exercise jurisdiction over international crimes unless there was a link with the victims of the crime. In some instances, states have ignored evidence of the presence of criminals from overseas in their territory, or declined requests to receive and prosecute such persons in their national courts. It has been argued that the new International Criminal Court will change this once it comes into existence. Because the Court can receive complaints from any source, including civil society organisations, it is very likely to refer a number of cases to states. States will then be faced with the choice of investigating and prosecuting cases themselves, or be seen as failing in their obligations to international justice as the case is added to the ICC's docket. Either way, we can expect to see an increase in the pursuit and prosecution of international criminals. As political leaders come to recognise that impunity for those who exercise power in a criminal fashion is increasingly improbable, they are less likely to resort to repression. Those megalomaniacs who wish to, will obtain little support from their adjutants. In this way, the exercise of international criminal law is likely to deter repressive regimes. The Pinochet effect is certain to be significant.

1   "South Africa—Ethiopia: Mengistu slips out", 8 December 1999,
    United Nations IRIN humanitarian information unit,
    http://www.reliefweb.int/IRIN.
2   Colum Lynch, "Iraqi Official Flees Austria—Alleged Role in Kurd Killings
    Spurs Criminal Complaint", *Washington Post*, August 19, 1999, at A18.
3   For an account of the principal mechanisms available for the protection of
    minority rights under international law, see Bernard F. Hamilton, "The
    Efficacy of International Minority Law", 88-91, in *Fresh Thoughts for
    Human Rights: A Report of the National Capital Area Division, United Nations
    Association of the United States of America*, (Washington DC, 1994)
4   See, for example, Gerald Segal, *The World Affairs Companion*, 60-67
    (London: Simon & Schuster, 1976).
5   S/RES/688 (1991) adopted by the Security Council at its 2982nd meeting
    on 5 April 1991.
6   U.N. Doc. A/64/Add. 1, p.188, Resolution 95 (I) of the General Assembly,
    11 December 1946.
7   1950 U.N. GAOR, 5th Sess., Supp. No. 12 (A/1316).
8   Article VI   "Persons charged with genocide or any of the other acts
    enumerated in Article III shall be tried by a competent tribunal of the State
    in the territory of which the act was committed, or by such international
    penal tribunals as may have jurisdiction with respect to those Contracting
    Parties which shall have accepted its jurisdiction."
9   Article 7 (1) "The State Party in the territory under whose jurisdiction a
    person alleged to have committed an offence referred to in article 4 is
    found shall in the cases contemplated in article 5, if it does not extradite
    him, submit the case to its competent authorities for the purpose of
    prosecution."
10 Marilyn August, Associated Press Writer, "French Court upholds
    conviction of Maurice Papon, Vichy official cited for role in Holocaust"
    Detroit News, October 21, 1999.
11 S/RES/827 (1993) on *Establishing an International Criminal Tribunal for the
    Prosecution of Persons Responsible for Serious Violations of International
    Humanitarian Law Committed in the Territory of the Former Yugoslavia since
    1991*, May 25, 1993.
12 S/RES/955 (1994) establishing the International Tribunal for Rwanda,
    November 8, 1994.
13 William Schabas "The Genocide Convention at Fifty" January 7 1999, US
    Institute for Peace *Special Report*. See
    http://www.usip.org/oc/sr/sr990107/sr990107.html
14 A/CONF.183/9, *Rome Statute of the International Criminal Court* adopted by
    the United Nations Diplomatic Conference of Plenipotentiaries on the
    Establishment of an International Criminal Court on 17 July 1998.
15 For a further discussion of the ICC see Bernard F. Hamilton, "New court
    offers new torture definition and new hope for victims", *Journal of
    International Law and Policy*, December 1998, (University of California,
    Davis).

SHARPENING THE WEAPONS OF PEACE

Philip Wilkinson

Some pacifists see no place for the military in peace work. But, as one Bosnian said to me after the deployment of IFOR, "At least we've stopped killing each other". In this chapter, Colonel Philip Wilkinson examines current British army thinking about Peacekeeping, in which light-armed troops police a ceasefire with the consent of the parties, and Peace Enforcement, which seeks to impose a cessation of violence.

The formulation of military doctrine for operations involving British troops, on behalf of the United Nations (UN) has been through several recent stages of development. In the immediate period following World War II, the UK did not become directly involved in UN activities—the 1950-53 war in Korea being the one major exception. The Cold War dominated British military thinking and doctrine, and consequently, British troops were focused on forward deployment in West Germany. In the run down of the British Empire (up until the 1960s), they were also engaged in countering insurgencies in Aden, Cyprus, Malaya and Palestine. At this time, the involvement of British troops in UN Peacekeeping Operations in Africa and the Middle East was minimal. Only after the Greek-Turkish crisis in Cyprus during 1963, and the more serious confrontation in 1974 did the UK become actively involved in UN Peacekeeping Operations. It was not until 1988 that the British Army developed and published its first Peacekeeping manual—entitled Army Field Manual (AFM), Volume V, Part 1, *Peacekeeping Operations*. The slowness in producing any doctrine for Peacekeeping can perhaps be partly explained by the British Army's traditional aversion to doctrine. But probably it was also a reflection of the prevailing mood, then and now, which is that peacekeeping is well within the competence of a full-time professional army. Dag Hammersjöld's oft quoted saying that "Peacekeeping is not a job for soldiers but only soldiers can do it" would not be a view subscribed to in the British Army when referring to 'traditional peacekeeping'. A more accurate expression of the British Army's attitude to 'traditional peacekeeping' might be that while soldiers make good peacekeepers not all peacekeepers make good soldiers. With the end of the Cold War and the greater involvement of British Forces in more complex UN operations, the development of the UK's doctrine for Peacekeeping has been dynamic. In 1994 the Army published Army Field Manual Volume 5, Part 2 *Wider Peacekeeping* in an attempt to address the more complex and dangerous challenges posed by on-going intra-state conflicts. *Wider Peacekeeping* was essentially a restatement of traditional peacekeeping doctrine (defined as "the wider aspects of peacekeeping operations carried out with the general consent of the parties but in an environment that may be highly volatile") albeit an attempt to stretch that doctrine to meet more difficult circumstances. *Wider Peacekeeping* did not address enforcement but recognised that there was a requirement to do so, and that doctrinal development in this area was highly dynamic, so it was issued as an "interim" publication only.

Since its publication, the doctrine in *Wider Peacekeeping* has been continuously revised, updated and developed as a joint (tri-service) statement to cover both Peacekeeping Operations and Peace Enforcement, collectively called Peace Support Operations. This new doctrine represents the experiences, lessons and predictions of more recent practitioners. It has been developed after wide international discussion involving not just military forces but also other partner civilian agencies. Concurrently various academic theses have identified changes in the strategic environment and tried to provide conceptual frameworks to embrace the new challenges and to address the gap between peacekeeping and war.

There is a debate within the military between the more traditionalist supporters of peacekeeping and war-fighting doctrines in their purest sense, and those who support a wider Peace Support Operations doctrine. It has been remarkably similar to the argument between the idealists and the consequentialists in the humanitarian community—those who believe they have a duty to do good things simply because they are good, versus those who measure the value of their actions against their wider consequences so that if it is necessary, for example, to deal with warlords and possible violators of human rights to save human lives, they will do so. *At this point, Peacekeeping turns into Peace Enforcement.* The harsh reality of operating in this conceptual and ethical 'grey area' between peace and war has been much debated. Perhaps this is not surprising given the nature of the individuals in the respective military and humanitarian communities. It is perhaps also not surprising, considering the corporate nature of the military, compared to the more disparate humanitarian community, that the military have been the first to enunciate a new doctrine for operations in the 'grey area'.

In defining this new doctrine, which accepts the necessity of "dining with the devil" if needs must, it has been necessary to develop a strong ethical base to the doctrine in order to try and avoid those moral dilemmas so corrosive to good morale. Accordingly, the new doctrine places considerable emphasis on the legal status of operations and promotes the use of International Humanitarian Law as the criteria against which all actions should be measured and judged. Similarly the new doctrine addresses the moral and legal dilemmas that may be faced by peacekeepers when confronted by human rights abuses but debarred by their Rules of Engagement from intervening. In Bosnia the UNPROFOR forces were unable to take action even when they witnessed high levels of violation. This became known as the 'bystander syndrome' and was highly damaging to military morale. So the Peace Support Operations doctrine draws a stark difference between Peacekeeping and Peace Enforcement, not in terms of conduct, but in legal authority and force capability. *Should it be likely that a military force be confronted by widespread human rights abuses it should be deployed with the legal mandate and resources to conduct enforcement from the outset. Other peace related operations such as conflict prevention, peace making and peace building are seen as principally the preserve of the diplomatic and humanitarian agencies, albeit closely supported by military forces.* For example military peacekeeping or even an early forward armed presence may deter conflict and support wider diplomatic conflict prevention activities.

A NATO document lists the following likely military tasks in peace support operations:

a. The control and verification of compliance with peace agreements, ceasefire agreements or armistices. **The exercise of control and the enforcement of compliance may require combat actions.**

b. Assistance to fulfilling agreements on peaceful settlements of a conflict.

c. Contribution to Conflict Prevention through preventive deployment.

d. **Guarantee or denial of freedom of movement.**

e. Conduct, supervise or support mine-clearing and explosive ordnance and improvised explosive reconnaissance and disposal, and mine awareness training programmes.

f. Demilitarisation or demobilisation operations, including those involving foreign military personnel.

g. Supporting humanitarian relief and assistance operations to civilian populations, including refugees.

h. Within the broad context of a Peace Support Operation eliminating human rights abuses and supporting the restoration of human rights.

i. Assistance in planning, monitoring and the conduct of elections.

j. Supporting the restoration of civil order and the rule of law, including the apprehension of war criminals.

k. Enforcement of sanctions and embargoes.

l. Assisting in the co-ordination of activities supporting economic rehabilitation and reconstruction.

Though the list does not make a sharp distinction between Peace Keeping and Peace Enforcement, the tasks which I have shown in bold type clearly could involve a degree of enforcement which UN Peacekeeping Forces have not generally been mandated to use.

I will now describe how British Peace Support Operations doctrine has developed since the end of the Cold War and offer an insight into Joint Warfare Publication 3-50 *Peace Support Operations* and the guidance that it offers military practitioners.

Army Field Manual Vol V Part 1 *Peacekeeping Operations* was designed to provide guidance for the conduct of traditional UN, inter-state Peacekeeping operations. The absence of any such publication prior to 1988 was probably a reflection of the low priority accorded to Peacekeeping Operations by the British Army. With its long and wide experience of counter-insurgency in the colonies, and in support of the Royal Ulster Constabulary in Northern Ireland, the British Army may have considered the relatively benign Peacekeeping operations of those days manageable without specific doctrinal guidance.

With the end of the Cold War the nature of Peacekeeping Operations has changed. Operations are now increasingly into volatile, high risk intra-state environments—such as Cambodia, Somalia, Bosnia. Such complex emergencies involving many different military and civilian agencies clearly do require a greater degree of doctrinal guidance than hitherto.

It was in response to an urgent operational requirement to meet the doctrinal needs of the UN Protection Force (UNPROFOR) in the former Yugoslavia, that the UK's Directorate of Land Warfare produced the Army Field Manual *Wider Peacekeeping*. This was designed specifically to offer guidance to the Armed Forces who were operating at the time in Bosnia and who were attempting to keep the peace in the midst of a civil war and when there was no peace to keep.

The perceived failures in UNPROFOR's mission were not due to a lack of military competence.   Rather, they resulted from insufficient political will and commitment from the international community. Although widely criticised, UNPROFOR achieved as much as could reasonably be expected, given its limited resources and mandate. (It is also generally acknowledged, in post operational assessments, that the *Wider Peacekeeping* manual provided the tactical guidance which prevented the British share of the operation from turning into a debacle.)   In the absence of any coherent policy there was no military alternative but to maintain the military operation with the hope that there would be some form of peace initiative at the political/strategic level, before the operation lost tactical credibility.   *In the longer term, military actions are no substitute for political initiatives. As a result, UNPROFOR could only put off the inevitable day when an operational commander would have to force the issue at the political level.* In mid-1995 UNPROFOR was confronted by what Lieutenant General Rupert Smith, commander of the UN forces in Bosnia, described as "the fork in the road" with UNPROFOR either becoming incredible and untenable or switching to Peace Enforcement. Wisely, the decision was to chose the Enforcement route and as a consequence provide fresh impetus to the political process.

With the benefit of hindsight, it is now generally considered that UNPROFOR was the wrong force, with the wrong mission for the circumstances which prevailed at the time in Bosnia.   Measured against the two truisms that you can not keep the peace unless there is a peace to keep (quoted from General Rose) and that you can not fight wars from white painted vehicles (quoted from General Smith), UNPROFOR clearly lacked the essential resources for the environment in which it was operating and the tasks that it was given. This has led to a re-examination of the *Wider Peacekeeping* Manual.   In the manual, the term "wider peacekeeping" was defined as "the wider aspects of peacekeeping operations carried out with the general consent of the parties but in an environment that may be highly volatile". *The view now is that Peacekeeping forces (which rely on consent) should not be deployed into a civil war involving widespread human rights abuses.*

Curtailment of these abuses may bring a general loss of consent which is beyond the ability of the peacekeepers to manage and risk the failure of the mission. These were the circumstances in which UNPROFOR found itself operating and which came to a head in mid 1995. In such circumstances the restriction of human rights abuses and other tasks requiring enforcement can only be accomplished, and should only be attempted, by a force capable of over-matching whatever level of opposition it may be offered.

Four years on from the issue of *Wider Peacekeeping* it is now considered that there is sufficient experience and consensus, both nationally and internationally to produce a new doctrinal approach for Peace Support Operations. This doctrinal approach acknowledges the critical participation of all three services, and also reflects the ever widening international military consensus that exists for the conduct of these operations. *Clearly, it makes little sense to produce a purely national doctrine for what are multi-national operations. Neither does it make good sense to produce a military doctrine for complex emergencies which does not reflect the wider involvement of civilian diplomatic and aid agencies. Success in Peace Support Operations requires the development of a composite strategy involving all agencies and parties.* So the developing doctrine has also been exposed to and discussed with a wide range of a civilian agencies with whom the military may operate on Peace Support Operations.

Work on this manual began with a re-evaluation of all previous UN Peacekeeping and enforcement operations (as then defined, such as the Korean and Gulf Wars), those "small wars" in which we had been involved in the draw-down of Empire, and our experiences in support to the civil power in Northern Ireland. The fundamental question that needed to be answered was, what was so different about modern operations in complex emergencies that merited a new doctrine? Peacekeeping and "war fighting" approaches had proved inappropriate, and the answer can be found when one examines more closely the desired outcome of a typical Peace Support Operation. Inevitably this will focus on security issues and the creation of a self-sustaining peace, not the defeat of a designated enemy. *Military actions must be designed to create a secure environment and conditions in which others can build a comprehensive and a self-sustaining peace, rather than a superficial termination of conflict by military force. Such a strategic requirement will require the combined efforts of a multitude of agencies and a very considerable commitment of resources.*

A key difference in more recent operations is that unlike traditional inter-state Peacekeeping operations where the parties are generally responsible and coherent actors, in a failing or failed state the parties may be ill disciplined, motivated by power and greed and indistinguishable from the rest of the population. Thus, any predictions of the levels of consent to intervention or other conditions may be so problematic as to be worthless. In which case, the judicious course of action would be to deploy with the necessary force levels to achieve the mission irrespective of any opposition—that is to prepare for Peace Enforcement from the outset.

I have quoted the two key lessons of UNPROFOR: wars cannot be fought from white painted vehicles, and peacekeeping cannot take place unless there is a peace to keep. *In more generic terms there is a minimum force level in relation to any potential opposition below which enforcement is not feasible and there is a minimum level of consent without which peacekeeping is not feasible.* Defining peacekeeping in terms of consent and force levels allows for a more precise examination of what lies in the "grey areas"—beyond peacekeeping by agreement, but short of war.

In the development of *Wider Peacekeeping* and other military doctrine of that time, there used to be an assumption that beyond Peacekeeping lay Peace Enforcement—and because Peace Enforcement was considered synonymous with war, war-fighting doctrine was sufficient for its execution. For example at that time the 1991 Gulf War was widely described as a Peace Enforcement operation. However, that is no longer the prevailing view. It is now generally understood that *military activities in Peace Support Operations are designed to create the conditions in which diplomatic and aid agencies can more effectively address the symptoms and underlying causes of the problem* and that these conditions are best achieved by employing a combination of coercion and inducements or a "stick and carrot approach". To do this effectively requires considerable military control and restraint, and co-ordination with the civilian agencies—they need to tell the military force what the conditions are that they would like created. This clearly justifies a comprehensive doctrine distinct from war fighting (while acknowledging that the ability to escalate and use combat remains a prerequisite in the Peace Enforcement planning)[*].

---

[*] The UK's new JP 3-05 "Peace Support Operations", NATO's new MC 327/1 "Military Concept for NATO Peace Support Operations" and FINABEL's paper T25R "Doctrine for Peace Support Operations" all start by defining a conceptual framework for Peace Support Operations which makes the distinction between Peace Support Operations and other more warlike operations, also conducted under Chapter VII of the UN Charter, before offering guidance for the conduct of Peace Support Operations.

Peace Support Operations are inevitably linked to the fundamentals of consent and impartiality and how these relate to the application of force. Peacekeeping is dependent on the consent of the parties, including the local citizens, and the promotion of co-operation and consent is fundamental for success. However the view that there is a "rubicon" of consent, which must not be crossed—as described in *Wider Peacekeeping*—is only relevant from the perspective of a lightly armed Peacekeeping force. For a Peace Support Operational force capable of combat, such as IFOR and SFOR in Former Yugoslavia, consent is an important consideration but it is a line which must be easily and frequently recrossed. *Indeed the ambition of a combat-capable Peace Enforcement force should be to lower its operational profile to that of peacekeeping as soon as is appropriate, while retaining its ability to escalate if necessary.* And these were the very conditions in which IFOR found itself on deployment to Bosnia in 1995/6. For such a force, a general loss of consent may be viewed as a tactical reverse, but it should not threaten the existence of the mission. However, if the conduct of all Peace Support Operations is designed to create a self-sustaining peace the promotion of co-operation and consent must remain a long term requirement.

The second most significant consideration concerned impartiality. The long-term requirement to build consent obviously demands an impartial approach to the conduct of operations. However, even if all Peace Support Operation actions are in support of an impartial mandate and conducted impartially will they be perceived that way? And does it matter if they are not? Impartiality is not neutrality, which suggests observation and passivity. *Impartiality requires a set of principles, generally enshrined in international humanitarian law and/or the mandate, against which the actions of the belligerent parties can be judged and acted upon.* Inevitably positive actions, whether the delivery of aid or the use of force, whether conducted impartially or not, will have consequences which penalise or favour one party more than another. Consequently Peace Support Operations activities will inevitably be seen as partial by one or other party at some stage of the operation and the force will be accused of bias. However, so long as the force's activities are driven purely by principled and clearly defined impartiality, such accusations can be refuted and the subsequent damage to consent eventually rebuilt. An analogy can help to explain this. The law does not designate an enemy—it simply states those conditions which must be maintained. And just as a criminal may perceive the policeman who "collars" him as being partial, so the Peace Support Operations force can expect to be accused of being partial by any party that does not comply with the operation mandate and experiences the consequences. But the impartial status of the law is not compromised because it penalises the guilty and protects the innocent. It is what motivates the policeman or Peace Support Operations practitioner that is most significant, not how he is perceived—at least in the short term.

So having restricted Peacekeeping doctrine to operations where there is a peace to keep, and having identified that Peace Enforcement is different from war and why, it has been possible to define Peace Enforcement and offer guidance for its conduct. The current doctrinal approach for Peace Enforcement is designed to offer commanders the maximum flexibility in the conduct of operations. In simple terms, it offers a wide range of enforcement and consent-promoting techniques; it suggests the use of enforcement where there is opposition and the use of consent-promoting techniques to maintain consent where it already exists, or to build consent where it is uncertain. As such the conduct of operations will rely heavily on good information and techniques designed to persuade the warring, or former warring factions, that their best interests lie in peace rather than a return to conflict. *When and if one of the warring parties fails to comply with the mandate and it be necessary for the Peace Support Operations force to use force, the aim would be to re-enforce the peace rather than the physical defeat of the non-complying faction.* The aim is to apply the most appropriate technique to grasp and maintain the initiative so as to increase consent at the expense of opposition and to create the greater operation space in which other civilian agencies (such as police, aid organisations, demining and reconstruction teams, and the civil authorities) can function.

Peace Support Operations doctrine requires that military commanders balance the short term advantages which may be gained from the use of enforcement techniques, with the requirements of diplomatic and aid agencies and the long term demands of peace. In addition, they must ensure that military efforts to build consent are co-ordinated into a wider multi-agency "hearts and minds" strategy. *Military actions are designed to conclude conflict by conciliation rather than a short term and superficial termination of the conflict by force. A stable and self-sustaining peace, not military victory, is the ultimate measure of success in Peace Support Operations.* Military forces may need to conduct combat operations to enforce compliance, but the use of force will be constrained by the long-term requirement to rebuild consent and peace building in general. And the new doctrine acknowledges that while peace building activities will be supported by information operations

and Civil Military Co-operation activities and projects the prime
responsibility for peace building rests with other civilian agencies.
The military view is that the most cost-effective use of scarce resources
can be achieved by the early development of a multi-agency strategy or
mission plan. This should draw together the activities of the various
agencies so as to achieve both unity of purpose and effort. This plan
will need to develop an entry strategy to co-ordinate the incremental
engagement of various agencies into the mission, to define lines of
operation, objectives, main effort, exit strategies and co-ordination
mechanisms. *It may well be that the main effort does not lie with the
military.* In the conduct of Peace Support Operations, military forces
must be prepared to be placed in support of a civilian agency or a
political 'supremo' who may be referred to as the Head of Mission or
possibly High Representative. It is the responsibility of this Head of
Mission to develop and co-ordinate the mission plan, not the military
force commander, although he will make a significant input into its
development.

In light of recent operations and many shared experiences and lessons
the international military community realised it had to develop a new
multi-national and multi-agency doctrine for the conduct of what are
now defined as Peace Support Operations. This process has required
monitoring, collating, analysing and discussing a wide range of
different national military and civilian experiences from the Lebanon,
Cambodia, Somalia, Bosnia, Rwanda &c. From this inter-action a
doctrine has been developed which is now shared by most of the major
players[*]. However, this must remain a dynamic doctrinal area because
as I said at the start of this article the doctrine that has been developed,
in particular for Peace Enforcement, is mainly predictive and has yet to
stand the test of operational reality!

---

[*] Initially the consensus was developed between partner nations, in particular
the UK, US and France but gradually that consensus spread to include
institutional bodies such as the FINABEL group of nations (France, Italy,
Netherlands, Allemagne, Belgium, Espagne, Luxembourg and now including
Greece, Turkey and Portugal), NATO and now the Nordic nations. It is this
international consensus which is now represented in many new national
doctrine publications, including the UK's new Joint Warfare Publication which
should be published shortly.

ON SIGNS, SIGNALS AND ACTION: PRE-EMPTING COLLECTIVE VIOLENCE

Judith Large

Government's excuse for declaring war is that it is now "inevitable". But, as this chapter shows in some detail, the word often conceals a host of neglected warnings and overlooked opportunities to develop peaceful alternatives.

The opponent of pure military intervention (such as the bombing of Kosovo) in situations of violent oppression is often put on a moral and intellectual precipice. "Don't you care," comes the accusation, "about the human rights abuse of Albanians in Kosovo?" "History proves..."(one is told), "that only brute force will defeat evil". On the contrary to the first charge, one may care sufficiently about human rights abuse (and human life) to ask what the consequences of bombing might be, how bombing the north of a country will protect people being assaulted in the south, and whether the outcome will really be better? As for history, it may be felt that a little bit of history in itself can be a dangerous thing (being, as is beauty, so much in the eyes of the beholder!)

This chapter will argue that there are multiple processes and factors which contribute to any "defining moment" which prompts military response. There are also choices along the way for external intervenors to influence events. It will also argue that if we narrow our options to force only, then we may stand in danger of destroying the very thing we had hoped to save. Finally, the result of relying only on organised aggression (as opposed to organised protection) can be that we defeat our own purposes, as in the NATO action in Former Republic of Yugoslavia in the name of "human rights". Here is a clear tragic case of what in English parlance is called "throwing the baby out with the bath water": the human rights protection premise of the bombing is negated by subsequent persecution and forced fleeing of Serbian and Romany citizens in the wake of returning Kosovars. Surveying the enormous costs of the NATO operation, and long term tasks ahead, Hugo Young asked "Was this wasteland really what we wanted? Is our indefinite presence a promise we want to repeat? Is the UN system really so bankrupt that another Nato operation is preferable to trying to shore it up?"[1]

Young makes the classic traditional distinction of pointing to a military alliance and to the United Nations for response. Pivotal as these are in our understanding of world politics, there are a myriad of other bodies, governmental and non-governmental, diplomatic and informal, which also wield influence and conduct international transactions. There are commercial, educational, and health networks, journalists, media people, bankers, religious bodies, organisations devoted to law, to science, to agriculture, to the arts. There are growing attempts to embody human rights and to both codify and enforce international criminal justice. There are citizens concerned with the community development or the welfare of children, environmental activists, and so the list goes on.

There will be signs and signals of impending violence against or between groups, and possible counteracting actions. But whereas dropping a bomb is a fairly straightforward and simple act, we are talking here of social and political complexity.   Situations need unravelling to reveal potential pressure points for countering repression. If we could "wind the clock back" for Nazi Germany, Rwanda, Kosovo, or East Timor, we would find that repressive violence does not appear in a vacuum, suddenly visible on a media or historical landscape.

Our task then, is 1) to recognise repressive violence as something which has developed over time and is not a sudden event, and 2) to see if there are patterns or factors which may be recognised and responded to before a seeming explosion of abuse, and 3) to adapt our thinking so that it is connected, imaginative, and above all anticipative rather than reactive.

Recognising repressive violence as having developed over time

Physical violence, (whether a fight between two men in the street or assault on the innocent in Kosovo or East Timor) is manifest and dramatically visible. It becomes a dramatic picture-frame of sorts for a given situation. In the domestic example it may appear to define a bully, or a grudge, a criminal or drunken incident. We define "reasonable force" as the means police or others may use to restrain such fighters, pull them apart, limit the damage they do to themselves or to others. In most of northern Europe or the West increasing attempts are now made to understand why the fight happened and what ways forward there might be. Is there an issue or dispute to be settled? Is there a substance abuse problem, a history of abuse, a lesson or punishment due (fine, imprisonment, community service?) and so on. We continually work to refine such interventions and the criminal justice system interacts with social services and psychologists as well as with police.

Many will groan if we try to broaden this picture to international affairs, but let's look at it for a moment. I know an American man who was a decorated war hero in the second world war. He always believed firmly that it was the necessary to fight, to defeat Hitler's regime and the genocide it unleashed. But he had a transcending experience, face to face with a German POW in the snow, when he suddenly sensed their joint humanity, and how forces larger than themselves had propelled them to that point of being acute enemies. After the war he studied history. He began to see the entire era in a different light, concluding that events needn't have culminated with world war. He looked at the way Hitler had played on German economic insecurity, how desperate inflation in the Weimar period could be traced back to post World War 1 reparations, how Jews, gypsies and communists were first made scapegoats and then targets for death. He saw junctures at which history might have taken different turns. Thinking back to the scenes such as Belsen, to bombed and burning civilians, to his own memories of friends being de-capitated in battle, he could only desperately hope "Never again", much as people did after the first world war.

Yet here we stand today, facing the legacy of Rwanda, Kosovo, East Timor, to name but a few of contemporary wars. How do we even begin to reorient our thinking? How do we make any difference at all?

Johan Galtung suggests that we start by considering visible and invisible forms of violence:

VISIBLE	**Direct violence**	
INVISIBLE	**Cultural violence**	**Structural violence**

Galtung distinguishes direct violence, physical and/or verbal, visible as behaviour. But human action does not come out of nowhere. There are roots. He points to two of these, a culture of violence (heroic, patriotic, patriarchal, etc.) and a structure that itself is violent by being too repressive, exploitative or alienating; too tight or too loose for the comfort of people.

A life-long scholar of human behaviour, Galtung rejects the popular notion that "violence is in human nature". (The anthropologist Margaret Mead did the same, writing an essay on *War as a Human Invention*.) The potential for violence, like love, is in human nature; but circumstances and choice condition the realisation of that potential. Violence is not like eating or sexing, found all over the world with slight variations. The big variations in violence are easily explained in terms of culture and structure: cultural and structural violence cause direct violence, using violent actors who revolt against the structures and using the culture to legitimize their use of violence as instruments.

Let's look at Kosovo. In early 1999 the massacre at Racak, Kosovo, suddenly highlighted for western observers a situation which had been deteriorating—not for months, but for over a decade. Howard Clark, who knows the area well, points out that "As far back as 1987, there were warnings of war in Kosovo, and of the dangerous resurgence of populist Serbian nationalism that was making Kosovo its most important cause. The fact that Serbia has only now gone to war in Kosovo has little to do with any foreign conflict prevention. Rather the self-restraint of the Albanian population provided an opportunity that was wasted."[2]

Whereas there was little known organised resistance to Hitler's rise—and trickles of information in the 1930s compared to the flows and deluges of today—the facts and developments in Kosovo have been there for all to see, in a glaring post-Dayton spot light, should we have cared to look. The 1974 Yugoslav constitution gave the Albanians a form of home rule inside Serbia and Yugoslavia by granting Kosovo "autonomous province" status, giving the Albanians considerable control over their own affairs. Milosevic purged the local communist leadership repeatedly and stripped the province of its autonomy in 1989-90 by staging a referendum in Serbia. Through the early 90s, Milosevic erected a police state built on ethnic apartheid in Kosovo. He played on deep insecurities in Serbia (among them economic) to scapegoat the Albanians. In fact, it was watching the oppression of the Albanians which further pushed Slovene and Croat nationalists to break away as states, fuelling their own stereotype of Serbian government monopoly and domination.

Milosevic stripped Kosovo of its previous autonomous status. The stated Serbian goal was to reclaim Kosovo, claimed as the cradle of Serbian civilisation and the site of the richest mines in the republic. This meant reversing progress Albanians had made in 15 years of autonomy, giving preference to the Serbian minority (by restoring Serbian privilege in employment), and attempting to redress the demographic balance. New measures were enacted. Serbs were forbidden to sell property to Albanians, factories were relocated to other parts of the republic, and some 127,000 workers (over 70% of Albanians in employment in Kosovo) were sacked. Meanwhile incentives were offered to those few Serbs and Montenegrins willing to settle in Kosovo.

The education system was identified as a source of the Kosovo Albanian cultural renewal and the university was seen as a nest of nationalism. Belgrade imposed a uniform Serbian curriculum for the whole republic. When Albanians refused to teach this, first they had their pay withdrawn, then police moved in to shut down schools and the university. The police force was expanded, Albanian police officers dismissed, and a variety of repressive tactics were used to humiliate the Kosovo Albanians or to provoke them to violence. As Clark observes, "In short, life in Kosovo took on the character of an occupation."

And yet a sophisticated Albanian system of alternatives took root, funded by taxes on the sizeable Albanian diaspora in the west, mainly in Germany and Switzerland. The "parallel" society was based on nonviolence and recalled Solidarity's experiment in passive resistance in Poland. In 1990 the Albanians declared Kosovo an "independent republic". By May 1992, just after the start of the Bosnian war, the Albanians organised their own Kosovo election to vote in a new parliament and government. They organised their own schooling, self-help, and social and medical care which included outreach to minorities in need (poor Serbs as well). By 1994-5 Bosnia was at the centre of international attention, and Kosovo was left to fester.

"This snub to the peaceful policy helped to radicalise the Albanians and spur the emergence of the militants in the form of the Kosovo Liberation Army. For the KLA, the lessons of Croatia and Bosnia were plain—force is the only language that Milosevic understands. Moreover, in the battle to enlist western support, peaceful resistance earns only sympathy, but no action."[3]

Reports on human rights violations in Kosovo were written and published. Serbian Orthodox monks in Kosovo spoke out when the first armed attacks began on Albanians, conducted by men well known to the war crimes court at the Hague and to citizens in Belgrade where they lived in high style. Appeals went out again and again in the early days of rising repression. In a similar way, appeals had gone out from Rwanda about impending mass murder—from evidence of hate propaganda to actual genocide plans leaked by a member of the government to the commander of UNAMIR, (a UN force which was present at the time) and sent by fax directly to the United Nations.[4]

After the Dayton agreement British banks sent delegations to do business in Belgrade, with no mention of anything happening in Kosovo. After the UNAMIR general desperately faxed the UN it was "business as usual" in New York, with no response forthcoming. British MP Ann Clwyd recommended to the Foreign Office in May 1999 that it was essential to disarm the militia in East Timor before a referendum on independence took place.[5] In each case there was obvious failure to separate out and respond to factors which would ultimately lead to the most horrific of violence.

Separating out trends or factors which contribute to violence

The repression of Albanian rights in Kosovo and the use of propaganda scapegoating them as enemies of Serbia are examples of trends which later converged in the form of organised physical violence. The same applied in Rwanda, with the added factor of an actual plan for genocide which was leaked by Rwandan sources (see above). It is surely a major challenge and acute responsibility to recognise such signs, to intervene when possible in situations which are obviously prone to violence. Such situations seem likely to include a volatile combination of any of the following:

economic crisis or political instability which exposes the general population to a degree of insecurity

a culture of authoritarianism or conformity

little diffusion or decentralisation of power (few checks and balances on decision making or control)

subordination or demonisation of one or more groups

denial of human rights with little external interference

no broad based media, communication or information flow

an atmosphere of expectancy or tension

mobilisation, or the organising of groups for violence.

These should be viewed as possible ingredients which may combine in varying degrees. All of them applied to the rise of Nazi Germany. All of them were equally relevant to Rwanda and to Kosovo where external response was too little too late. They are equally relevant to Indonesia's current acute problems of Aceh, Ambon, as well as its response to the referendum in East Timor, a tragedy of massive proportions.

The unleashing of hate propaganda is something which many contemporary sectors recognise and attempt to counteract—journalists, teachers, writers of story song, play or film, performers, human rights groups, television and radio media people can all play a role in attempting to highlight or counteract the demonising of an identity group. The potential use of local independent radio is now recognised in Burundi, Rwanda and the Balkans for this purpose. Philip Gourevitch, in his profound study of stories from Rwanda, quotes Ralph Ellison's *Invisible Man* : "Beware of those who speak of a spiral of history; they are preparing a boomerang. Keep a steel helmet handy."[6]

It is noteworthy that under the Nazi regime in the 30's, and more recently in Rwanda and in Yugoslavia (as above) a particular party line was pushed heavily about a chosen people's destiny, about the inferiority of another people, and justification for violent "solutions" cloaked in historical language. The evocation of the German master race, and the legacy of the "Volk" were used to demonise the Jews. Tutsis were known in Rwanda as "Inyenzi", which means cockroaches, and the Biblical myth of Ham was cited by Hutu leaders when they called for the deportation of all Tutsis back to Ethiopia, before they started killing them. Extremist Serbian leadership harked back to 14th century battles in proclaiming their grudge against Muslim Albanian Kosovars. There was indeed a "boomerang" in all of these situations.

Another aspect held in common in these examples is the centralisation of power. Gourevitch was told the following in Rwanda: "Conformity is very deep, very developed here. In Rwandan history, everyone obeys authority. People revere power, and there is not enough education. You take a poor, ignorant population, and give them arms, and say *It's yours—Kill*. They'll obey. The peasants, who were paid or forced to kill, were looking up to people of higher socio-economic standing to see how to behave. So the people of influence, or the big financiers, are often the big men in the genocide—the people were looking to them for orders."[7]

Almost identical words were said to me in northern Serbia in late 1992, by a young peace activist desperate to describe the urban/rural divide and authoritarian values in his country. There was dissent in the urban areas, particularly among intellectuals and youth, there was even dissent in the army. But the strong rural backbone of the country provided unstinting support for the regime. And why not? Illiteracy was fairly high. There was no exposure to democratic traditions of choosing leadership, of accountability or participation. People no doubt had memories of brutal treatment for those who did not obey. They had no information to counter state/official broadcasting. They had no precedents for challenging central power.

What then, can we say about the use of power in repressive regimes? Gourevitch puts it this way: "I said earlier that power largely consists in the ability to make others inhabit your story of their reality, even if you have to kill a lot of them to make that happen. In this raw sense, power has always been very much the same everywhere; what varies is primarily the quality of the reality it seeks to create: is it based more in truth than in falsehood, which is to say, is it more or less abusive of its subjects? The answer is often a function of how broadly or narrowly the power is based: is it centred in one person, or is it spread out among many different centres that exercise checks on one another? And are its subjects merely subjects or are they also citizens? In principle, narrowly based power is easier to abuse, while more broadly based power requires a truer story at its core and is more likely to protect more of its subjects from abuse."[8]

Communications and education work, empowerment for reform, can take a long time. It took centuries in our own European history to move from subjects to citizens. What if the situation is critical, urgent, as in Kosovo in the spring of 1999?

Note Gourevitch's definition of power, "the ability to make others inhabit your story of their reality". What if the War Crimes Tribunal and western officials who already knew that Arkan (for example) was leading paramilitaries to plunder Kosovar Albanians in the summer of 1998 had named him then, placing him right in their story of war crimes reality? Why was his complicity revealed in our newspapers months later, well into the bombing campaign, as though sudden discovery had just been made? What if bankers in Belgrade had linked their financial talks or deals to change in the human rights situation in Kosovo, i.e. "If you do this, we would consider doing this…" or what is called *conditionality*. Would there, could there have been leverage, incentive for change?

Finally, it is possible to mobilise for peace just as it is possible to mobilise for war. War and collective violence require enormous co-operation and co-ordination. Gourevitch says it beautifully: "Genocide, after all, is an exercise in community building. In 1994 Rwanda was regarded by much of the rest of the world as the exemplary instance of the chaos and anarchy associated with collapsed states. In fact, the genocide was the product of order, authoritarianism, decades of modern theorizing and indoctrination, and one of the meticulously administered states in history."[9]

It is possible to counter-mobilise, to organise meticulously for non-violence. Witness the work of groups such as the Osijek Peace Centre in Croatia, whose members occupied the house of targeted minorities who were to be evicted and deported, who organised festivals promoting non-violence and "another way" in the midst of war. Witness the massive popular ground swell, the "people power' which led to the downfall of repressive regimes in eastern Europe, or the concerted effort of community groups and townships in South Africa who worked against the odds to reverse a possible tide towards civil war and achieve democratic elections. Witness, belatedly, the valiant attempts of the Albanian non-violence movement to secure external recognition and allies for peaceful change.

July 1991 saw the launch of the charter of the Anti-War Campaign, written in Zagreb and signed by both individuals and organisations. By the end of the year, 76 groups and organisations from ex-Yugoslav republics signed the charter and about 500 individuals. Movement for Peace and Non-violence from Ljubljana (Slovenia), the Sarajevo Peace Centre of Civil Forum (Bosnia and Herzegovina), the Titograd Peace and Civil Committee (Montenegro) were among the signers. In this way the Charter became the basis of an unofficial gathering of peace activists against war in Croatia and other regions. A "basic information." document published the Antiwar Campaign Council, Croatia in February 1992 stated the following:

"With the escalation of the war in Yugoslavia, peace initiatives in all republics started to take place in July last year. They emerged spontaneously, were organised in various ways and started numerous actions... All these groups and organisations are facing the same problems: political pressure by the authorities and warmongering political parties and movements (especially pronounced in Serbia), the media blockade, the lack of knowledge and experience and the lack of money and other material facilities. Apart from that, war operations aggravate communication exchange considerably (traffic blockade, the blockade of telephone and mail exchange). The Campaign is also faced with various problems due to different political attitudes which we try to overcome by our common principles of non-violence, democracy, co-operation and the right of dissimilarity."

Among the initial projects were: Training for non-violence, conflict resolution and mediation, the publication of a newsletter called *ARKzin,* research into "war in the media" and *Peace Entrance*—an open-air stage for concerts and happenings, human rights protection, war crime research, and the development of policies for peace and demilitarisation. Other focus areas included support for the right of conscientious objection and alternatives to military service, organising volunteers to help with post-war reconstruction, enabling women's empowerment and protest organisations, translation of literature on non-violence, and "re-socialisation" of former soldiers (with help from Vietnam Veterans Against War, USA). The Belgrade Centre operated along similar lines.[10]

Adapting our thinking to be anticipative rather than reactive

On the eve of the NATO bombing of Serbia tension ran very high in European countries, pushed to tangible proportions by press releases and the "CNN factor". There was an enormous ultimatum at hand.

Either "the Serbs" gave in to NATO demands on Kosovo or NATO would bomb them, to quote many an observer, "back to the stone age". It was the ultimate in threats, a devastatingly clear *either/or* dichotomy. Or was it?

The implication was that the West was either to bomb or "do nothing". Not bombing was equated with doing nothing, and by and large as a public we were lulled into this dominant thinking. The word "appeasement" was used repeatedly on the media for those who were against bombing. "Unity" was required, if I remember correctly, by a British Labour government which had criticised Milosevic for not allowing dissent.

Here is a false logic which troubles me greatly. Bombing was never seriously an option in our dealings with a repressive apartheid regime in South Africa, was it? Or did I miss something? And yet a massive flow of activities, contacts, and measures were put in place to change that regime. No one can tell me that "we did nothing". The flow to Eastern Europe in the 1970s and 80s of ideas and images, church and human rights activists, academics and business people, brought down the Berlin Wall in a far more effective way than bombs.

I was in Pristina in February 1999 working with health groups. The tensions were extremely high. It was my impression that people did expect war, but that they expected conventional war between the Yugoslavian Army and the Kosovo Liberation Army. They expected it because a situation of oppression was now out of control, and no one had listened to them five years, eight years earlier. Trust had broken down terribly, and ordinary Albanians had no channels of expression to ordinary Serbs living in Serbia. In Kosovo itself the extremists in each group put pressure on people not to mix with the "other". And there was pain, the pain of killings and reprisals and fear. Finally, they expected war, because they had little faith in the leadership of both sides at talks in France convened by outside powers.

So on the eve of the bombing, I thought of these people, of their insecurity, and wondered out loud, "What will happen to the Kosovar Albanians when NATO begins bombing Serbia? Won't anger be vented on them even more?" Of course it was, and two months later the following account was published in a daily paper:

> Meli always feared what would happen if the west intervened with force, saying it gave licence to the Serbs to take revenge on the majority Albanians here. "I didn't expect this to happen; I didn't want Nato to bomb, but it happened," she said. "I knew if they

started to bomb it would be very bad for the people here, and I was really afraid of the paramilitaries and the crazy Serbs, because they knew just what they wanted to do and they did it. I think it was all written down."[11]

Were we really surprised that refugees fled in their thousands? How could we be? When politicians say "It would have happened anyway, we bombed to prevent a humanitarian disaster", how can they believe their own words?

Finally, what can we say to opposition groups, to alternative voices for change in Serbia, who felt the tirade of our mass weaponry, who were labelled "the enemy within", who lost loved ones, bridges, heating water, and any trust they may have held for the West. Activists who struggled there before to change authoritarian educational methods, to introduce ideas of participation, human rights and democratisation, or to fight prejudice, must now struggle to have warmth and shelter in the coming winter. Our newspapers do not seem to cover the exodus of Serbs from Kosovo when the tide of revenge turned . Nor do we read of the enormous toxic pollution caused by the bombing of petro-chemical plants.

Bombing was highly reactive behaviour, and to me this policy held little anticipative thinking apart from the priority of saving western lives and only using hardware to smash another people. If we queried the results, outcomes and consequences of our own actions, we might better prevent deaths and repression. What would the result be of withdrawing UNAMIR from Rwanda, of ignoring information on planned genocide? What could unarmed UN election monitors do in East Timor amid a highly armed Indonesian (anti-independence) military presence?

There is a lot of talk about "early warning" and "conflict prevention". Violence prevention, like preventative medicine, is hard to measure. Or is it?

Warren Zimmermann claimed that "The West was a prisoner of what could be called *the paradox of prevention.* In the Yugoslav case, as in many other international situations, it is nearly impossible to mobilize governments to take risks for prevention, since it is impossible to prove that the events which are to be prevented will, in the absence of prevention, occur."[12] But he is taken to task by another critic who asks in what sense was the West, and the United States in particular, really "a prisoner" of this paradox—particularly since no evidence exists that either the President or any other principals recognized that there was at least a need to "take risks for prevention" in the first place?[13]

Indeed, for missed opportunities in prevention we can look right back to the denial of debt relief to the Markovic government of Yugoslavia in 1990. Ante Markovic was committed to democracy, a civil society, and even a market economy. In a more sensible world American officials might have seen impending divisive nationalism as a threat to be averted with aid rather than a disqualification for receiving it. This would have been anticipative thinking.

Most of us do not walk the corridors of power or make decisions about debt or arms sales. But all of us can seek to weigh up the consequences of our own actions and choices. We can voice opinion and put pressure on decision makers. We can reach out through a variety of initiatives to other people across borders, to build links of support, mutuality, advocacy for change—debt relief, Amnesty campaigns, UN reform, relief or development projects, cultural or scientific initiatives, inter-faith dialogue, women's groups, war veterans or students. We can retain the ability to question and raise awareness.

In the words of Edward Said, scholar and Palestinian representative (writing during the NATO bombing of Serbia): "Unfortunately there are no quick solutions, no ready-made tactics to replace the prevailing logic of false dichotomies or an exacerbated sense of endangered identity. But by raising awareness of what the media at present distorts and hides, we can at least begin to stiffen our resistance to the direction and the leadership offered by men either like Milosevic or like Clinton, who has never experienced war or any of its terrible dislocating effects, and is drunk on the miracles of high-tech electronic warfare where you do not see or come anywhere near what your victims are suffering."[14]

The only answer is not to refuse to look at the endless pictures of refugees, but to develop the resistance that comes from a real education—patient and repeated criticism, and intellectual courage. Identity politics, nationalist passions and murderousness, an aggravated sense of victimhood or a saviour complex cannot be dealt with in any other way: these are universal problems requiring universal solutions, not spontaneous war or unreflecting quick fixes.

Annual world expenditure on military preparedness is currently estimated to be $800 billion.[15] How much of this contributes to real human security ? How much of it is sheer destructive fire-power? Is protective peacekeeping, on the ground, resisting thuggery and aggression, really enhanced by B52 or stealth bombers? Are new definitions of security and human needs now overdue, for preventing the disintegration or resort to violence? How long before we realise that the bombing of Iraq, the bombing of Serbia, does not bring about the finer qualities of tolerance or humanitarian values, does not immediately end an unpopular regime or better the lives of the population in question.

Let us never lose our compassion for suffering and willingness to respond. But let us also cultivate an awareness and sensitivity to signs and signals, and take imaginative and strategic actions to pre-empt collective violence, to protect the vulnerable, to build different futures. It is a longer, slower path than the use of only force, but it will lead to hope and renewal rather than destruction and retribution.

1   The Guardian, 8 June 1999, p.18
2   Howard Clark 'What happened to the nonviolent option?' NPC Newsletter October 1998 p. 6
3   Ian Traynor 'Political snubs that bred militants' The Guardian Thursday March 25 1999 p.3
4   *Early Warning and Conflict Management*, volume 2 of the Joint Evaluation of Emergency Assistance to Rwanda 1996. See also Philip Gourevitch, *We Wish to Inform you that tomorrow we will be killed with our families*, Picador 1999 pp. 104-106.
5   Ann Clwyd: *Another Rwanda* The Guardian, Sept. 8 1999. p.19
6   Gourevitch, p. 45
7   Gourevitch, p. 23
8   Gourevitch, p. 181
9   Gourevitch, p. 95
10 The previous three paragraphs are taken from my book *The War Next Door* (Stroud: Hawthorne, 1998)
11 Steven Erlanger *Trapped in tragic home*: report from Pristina in The Guardian Friday May 14 1999 p.4.
12 Warren Zimmermann, 'Yugoslavia: 1989-1996', in Jeremy Azrael and E. Payin, editors, *US and Russian Policy Making with Respect to the Use of Force* (Rand Institute, 1996), pp. 185-186
13 Mark Danner *The US and the Yugoslav Catastrophe*. The New York Review November 20, 1997 p.62.
14 Edward Said: *Forced to accept false logic* in Al-Ahram Weekly, 29April-5 May 1999
15 Karen Lifton, *Environmental Security & Ecological Interdependence*, Global Governance, vol.5 no.3, 1999. p. 373

UNOFFICIAL PEACE WORK:
SOME EXPERIENCES UNDER APARTHEID

John Lampen

As South Africa became increasingly polarised, the attention of the world focused on the drama of the freedom struggle. But confrontation without attempts at mediation and reconciliation is likely to spiral into more and more direct violence. In apartheid South Africa, as in Palestine, Sri Lanka, Northern Ireland, the former Yugoslavia and other places of conflict, there were unofficial and often unrecognised peace workers looking beyond victory and trying to build a new and peaceful society.

The larger factors which brought apartheid to an end are clear—the contradictions between such a policy and the needs of a modern industrial state; the education, empowerment and radicalisation of the oppressed communities; international disapproval, sanctions and disinvestment; the disappearance of the Portuguese colonies and the white Rhodesian regime, and the collapse of communism; the encouragement given by P.W. Botha's limited reforms—and the frustration when he then halted them, declaring a State of Emergency and trying to crush all opposition. Yet none of these factors explains why the repression melted away, instead of being overthrown by violence as so many people expected. I do not wish to exaggerate the importance of unofficial actors, one element among so many; but, as Sheena Duncan, for many years the National Director of Black Sash, told me:

> Challenges to unjust rule …were conducted by people with no official standing and were very much the combined effort of small voluntary groups which in 1983 combined under the umbrella of the United Democratic Front. Not all of these small groups joined the UDF but all of us supported its aims… Different voluntary groups focused on different pillars [supporting the structure of injustice] and they crumbled one by one.

Black Sash was an organisation of white women demanding civil rights for black people and protesting at abuses. I saw many examples of their work: one was to set up a rota of white observers to monitor one of the courts dealing with black people who had infringed the infamous "pass laws". There were many other groups which tried to bring injustice to light: among these, the South African Institute of Race Relations researched and published meticulous and unchallengeable data on the situation. The Centre for Intergroup Studies at Cape Town University (now the Centre for Conflict Resolution) promoted constructive and co-operative approaches to conflict resolution. PACSA in Pietermaritzburg and Diakonia in Durban worked to mobilise Christians of different races in a shared search for justice and community. The South African Council of Churches, committed to peace, justice and nonviolence under the leadership of Desmond Tutu, and later Beyers Naudé and Frank Chikane, was considered such a threat that the police secretly destroyed their office in Johannesburg with a bomb.

All these bodies had racially mixed staffs, (though inevitably their funding came from the white community and overseas donors), so there were tensions within the teams which pointed to a need for mutual understanding and reconciliation. In their work and witness too they found that protest and exposure was not enough; they felt impelled to run humanitarian and reconciliation projects. The Institute of Race Relations, for example, provided extra tuition classes for black school students, and was involved with "Operation Hunger".

But that is not to say that everyone agreed on the need for reconciliation. The Kairos Document, published by a group of leading Christians in 1986, said, "Any form of peace and reconciliation that allows the sin of injustice and oppression to continue is a false peace and counterfeit reconciliation".[1] Alan Boesak wrote:

Too long have Christians [in South Africa] attempted to avoid genuine reconciliation by proclaiming a "unification" that rests on a cloaking of guilt and a pious silence about evil. Too long they have tried to achieve reconciliation through apartheid, as if the two did not stand diametrically opposed to one another. Let us be honest about this: reconciliation is not holding hands and singing "Black and White Together". Reconciliation is not blacks and whites going to summer camp together…where we set aside apartheid and live in fellowship "in the Spirit" for a month, and then return to our separate life-styles. Reconciliation is not merely "feeling good", but doing what is right. [2]

Some thinkers have seen conflict as a necessary response to a negative situation. Only when life becomes intolerable for the top dogs, they say, will a settlement emerge; so reconciliation is an attempt to blunt the cutting edge of the problem, deferring a true resolution. The Kairos Document says:

> In our situation in South Africa today it would be totally unChristian to plead for reconciliation and peace before the present injustices have been removed. Any such plea plays into the hands of the oppressor by trying to persuade those of us who are oppressed to become reconciled to the intolerable crimes that are committed against us.

The work of groups within the oppressed community usually focused on education, community development and the struggle for freedom. But in retrospect, one can see that the work of the reconcilers moved hand in hand in hand with the work of protest. And in fact the situation was so complex, containing so many issues, that there was unlikely to be a single, simple way forward. Hugo van der Merwe wrote:

> A recognition of this multi-dimensionality should sensitise us to the limitations of specific approaches that only offer partial solutions, and which therefore need to be complemented by other intervention techniques. The complexity of the South African situation cannot be overemphasised when intervention processes are evaluated.[3]

Personal change

One of the most striking changes in South Africa was the way that the moral basis of apartheid was eroded; people who had accepted it entirely began to doubt and question. Such change is not produced by violence; it comes from a personal change of heart. H.W.van der Merwe (an Afrikaner, the Director of the Centre for Intergroup Studies and father of Hugo) explained that, while he was a teenager, his older brother used the word *vrou* of one of their servants. He had only heard that word applied to white women; "You mean *meid*," he said. "No, I mean *vrou*," said his brother. "That moment changed my whole life," he told me. The basis for conversion is often a human relationship; if a peace-builder wants to convert an opponent, the first step is to build rapport. Will Warren, a Quaker peace worker in Northern Ireland, said,

> I'm certain that it was only because I treated [the paramilitaries] as friends that I had any influence on them at all. Obviously the converse is also true. They had an influence on me to the extent that they treated me as a friend. That is how reconciliation works.

Steve Biko enjoyed telling a story of when he picked up two white hitchhikers on a drive to Johannesburg. At first they claimed to be English-speaking, but in the end admitted they were Afrikaners. Asked why they denied it, they said, "Well, we know that black people don't like Afrikaners." Biko told them never to deny their identity: "There's nothing to be ashamed of in language or culture. You should be proud of these things!" And for the rest of the long drive they chatted comfortably in Afrikaans. Sensitively, he avoided the topic of racial politics, saying later, "It would have been too traumatic, really. As it is they lost a fair amount of their racial prejudice on the trip without my having to work too hard at it!"[4]

One may reach out to one's enemies in very adverse circumstances. Rommel Roberts, a so-called "coloured" peace worker in Cape Town, described to me how he was detained in solitary confinement.

> There was my prison guard. He would scream at me to wake up at 5.00 in the morning and shove my food under my door. I started singing as he approached, hoping to start a little seed of communication. It took time. But eventually he would grunt a sort of "good morning"...

> Then there was a definite point when he saw me as human. Suddenly he saw my conditions. He was embarrassed and ashamed. But still, he was trapped. Prison regulations stifled his impulses, but there we some things he could do for the fellow man he saw in me. He could improve my food. He began sharing his own food with me. He slipped in a couple of extra blankets. We talked.

> I reflected on this in the light of the complex situation in South Africa. Maybe the approach I had used in this micro-conflict was valid for the macroscale. I came to feel that we who believe we see the light need to be able to absorb the viciousness of the "oppressor". We need to unlock his humanity.

The system of apartheid deliberately created barriers to communication. Chris Spies was a Dutch Reformed Mission Church minister in a small "coloured" community in a rural South African town. He was deeply involved in their development—too much so for the local white community, who were very suspicious of him. On a visit to Northern Ireland in 1989 he had several conversations with people who had crossed invisible boundaries to get to know their "enemies". Five months after his return, he wrote to me:

> Our approach has changed in the sense that we have tried to enter into meaningful and frank discussions with leaders like the mayor,

the town clerk and officials of the "white" church. In all the cases it proved to be very fruitful and, let us say, successful. The mayor himself was very happy and relieved after our discussions. In the end he came to watch our projects and he spent the morning with us in our house (which is in itself a courageous act in Burgersdorp) and he has promised to promote direct communication instead of allowing rumours to be spread around, in his words, "by people who claim to get their information directly from the security police". I now realise I neglected this basic biblical way of dealing with people in the past.

A particular problem for Chris was the local special branch police officer, who was trying to undermine him; for example, by anonymous letters in the local newspaper read by whites, and by telling black students that Chris had given him information about them. Chris considered going to talk with him personally, but his church council preferred to invite the officer's superior to a meeting. Soon the man was transferred, and the senior officer wrote a letter distancing the police from his actions. No more letters appeared in the paper.

1990 was a difficult year, in which the white Dutch Reformed Church in the town withdrew all financial support from the "coloured" congregation, and made moves to sell the minister's house. Rumours about Chris persisted, but in August he could report

> On several occasions have we gone to talk to the SA Police Chief in Burgersdorp. We have reached, in our opinions, a breakthrough. The police agreed to accept me as a mediator and facilitator. We've already had a very fruitful workshop with the police and the residents' association. Because the police has started to trust me and to develop an understanding that the leaders in the black community are not their enemies but a source for peace, they asked our help to restore calmness in the townships. In the near future we plan to facilitate the forming of an informal discussion group, consisting of key individuals in all the communities. This group will keep a low profile with no publicity. We would rather lay the eggs without cackling than cackle without laying eggs.

Mediation and Facilitation

The same approach can be attempted with leaders. Gandhi's relations with Jan Smuts are a famous example. When opposition leaders do not have direct access to one another, the task may be attempted by a

mediator.   In *Tools for Transformation* Adam Curle transcribes
examples of such discussions, with a comment:

> [The mediators] don't do this...by telling leaders what they ought
> to do; they are not qualified to do this either by role or by
> sufficient understanding of the needs of a nation or group.   What
> they can do, however, is to try to remove or put into perspective
> exaggerated fears and suspicions, to dispel rumours, to explain that
> what their enemies say is not necessarily what they mean, to argue
> that they are not the utter monsters they are imagined to be, in fact
> to change the perceptions of leaders to the point where they come
> to think that it may perhaps be worth entering into serious
> negotiations.[5]

H.W.van der Merwe, who helped to arrange meetings between the
ANC-in-exile and groups of Afrikaner students and later businessmen,
felt that the word "mediation" promised (or threatened) too much in
that context.   Indeed he told me that face-to-face meetings sometimes
increased animosity between those attending—but there was a gain in
accurate perception of each other.

> I have always maintained that I served as a facilitator assisting both
> parties to have meaningful communication and gain reliable
> information.   I did not urge the parties to put the knowledge to
> good use or to make peace...   The facilitator is less likely than the
> mediator to be seen as a meddler or a busybody, a preacher or a
> conciliator.[6]

This distinction is clear in a comment by Eddie Makue of the Justice
and Social Ministries of the South African Council of Churches:
"Rather than mediators being neutral, their credibility was derived
from the moral stance against whatever creates and fuels conflict. ...If
the primary objective is to resolve conflict, those who mediate should
have a proven commitment to this ideal."

Sheena Duncan recalled her first encounter with this sort of process in
1978, when she attended

> ...one of the many conferences organised outside South Africa to
> bring South Africans of all political persuasions together around
> one table on neutral territory.   Later on the mediation became all-
> important and it was entirely done by the voluntary and unofficial
> groupings—mainly the churches but also IDASA.

Other kinds of mediation were developing in the black African
community.   For example the Community Mediators in Guguletu
township were trained local people who offered a free service, and

intervened with a measure of success in the Cape Town "taxi war". Eddie Makue wrote to me:

> In a society where peacemakers were considered as enemies of the state, peacemaking processes were often clandestine and necessitated small workable entities. Such groups were voluntary and community based, often within traditional structures. Especially in rural communities, what are called "makgotlas" (traditional courts) are respected peacemaking mechanisms. During the time (1983–1989) when the legitimacy of the courts of law was in disrepute, Civic Associations utilised the existing Street Committees to resolve conflict. These structures evolved as an organic component of a political strategy aimed at isolating the official structures of government.

In 1987 President P.W.Botha allowed the white lawyer Richard Rosenthal to set up secret meetings between one of his ministers and Thabo Mbeki of the ANC to explore possible ways forward[7]. They reached a qualified agreement on the desirability and feasibility of a future negotiation process, which greatly strengthened F.W. de Klerk's position when he replaced Botha with a peacemaking mandate.

In summer 1991 a delegation of religious leaders met with President de Klerk to try to break the deadlock between the ANC and the government over dealing with nationwide outbreaks of violence. Business leaders and the Zulu party Inkatha were drawn into the discussions. The outcome was the National Peace Accord, officially launched in September to prevent and resolve violent political conflict at neighbourhood level, with the co-operation of security forces, administration, politicians and community groups. In many cases it prevented an escalation of violence which would have seriously damaged prospects of peace; it also gave organisations on different sides of the conflict their first experience of working as equals for the common good. The experience of the Makgotlas and Street Committees was crucial in giving black people a proper voice in the Regional and Local Peace Committees. Sheena described the unofficial mediators' role:

> The Peace Accord involved church leadership in endless meetings and shuttle diplomacy. The Peace Accord eventually became "official" but the unofficial and voluntary push and shove was essential to its success. It would not have worked at all without the voluntary involvement of very small community groups and ecumenical parish level commitment, as well as the dedication of small secular NGOs. The whole official negotiating process was

kept on track through crisis after crisis by the unofficial pressure groups. This commitment carried over into the preparations for the 1994 elections.

H.W. Van der Merwe wrote:

While coercion (including violence) and co-operation (including negotiation) stand in a relationship of tension towards each other, they are not mutually exclusive. In South Africa there was a clear need for coercive measures aimed at empowering the weaker party and at changing an unjust system. In the heat of the polarised debate the option of negotiation was often seen as contradicting the "struggle"... This however is a misconception. Negotiation should be seen as complementing pressure in the communication process between conflicting parties. By improving the quality of communication and understanding, negotiation will ensure more rational and effective pressures and more orderly change, so reducing the likelihood of destructive violence[8].

A Reconciliation Project

The South African struggle was so polarised that reconciliation work was often unpublicised, and its effects in averting a bloody outcome hard to measure. The actions of some whites who identified with the freedom struggle at heavy personal cost were known. It was not always politically expedient to acknowledge the far larger number who—within the unjust system—accorded black people assistance, respect and personal dignity. They certainly contributed to reconciliation and helped to justify the conciliatory spirit of the ANC. I want to describe one single example of a reconciliation project which shows the contribution of unknown people and questions the sharp distinction in the Kairos Document.

Koinonia South Africa was founded by Dr Nico Smith, an Afrikaner theologian, who left the (white) Dutch Reformed Church to join the (black) Dutch Reformed Church of Africa in a township congregation outside Pretoria. The essence of Koinonia's programme was the "meal group" of two black and two white couples who had a meal together once a month for six months in each other's homes. Usually, two of the couples had already been in a group, the others not.

The first meeting is usually uncomfortable, with a lot of staring. Here it is very important for each of the couples to simply share their life journey, their family life, their background and so on.

The power that is in sharing shows itself at this first meeting... It becomes a way of healing the deafness imposed by apartheid[9].

The participants had to cope with social embarrassments such as the contrast in lifestyle, and neighbours' curiosity.

The second meeting is dedicated to the sharing of spiritual journeys... This enables members of the meal group to discover and experience the richness of religious life that is integral to our communities. At the same time [they] feel and must deal with the estrangement that has been introduced into every area of religiosity or spirituality. This might be the first time a "black" or "white" person might ever have heard how an "Indian" sees relationship with God. This is the beginning of healing the division that has been made between the communities of South Africa in the very deepest, most meaningful area of their life.

Over the third meal the couples are able to share their views of the South African situation—social, political, economic, &c... The objective is not to indoctrinate, convince or create argument, but to allow each member to share their views of the problems and realities of South African life... The following meeting...builds on the previous evenings spent together by letting each person express his or her hopes, dreams and desires for the future of South Africa.

For the fifth and sixth month, the group visits a restaurant, a cinema, a church, &c. It is important to begin to extend the friendship and venture out into a black or white community, which requires that trust and compassion be present between the couples.

After the sixth meeting the four couples were encouraged to form new groups—without breaking the friendships already established. One participant said, "There is often an emancipation and a release from a bondage that had only been dimly realised before. The power in changing one's actions, and so one's experience, and its efficacy in changing our attitudes and our willingness to express our care, is inexpressible." Another wrote to his local paper: "As a white person, my Atterbridgeville [township] experience was an eye-opener, even though that may sound like a cliché. Never before have I been exposed to such poverty and harsh living conditions. Never before have I had to cope with that kind of fear... It hurts a lot."

This project reduced hostility and misperceptions, and increased mutual understanding, which prepared for change. But it did not obscure or postpone the issues which must be addressed—it highlighted them. This view was clearly shared by the right-wing

white group who sprayed the home of Ivor Jenkins, Koinonia's
Director, with bullets and the police who raided Koinonia's offices.
Nico Smith's own credentials in relation to the South African struggle
were impeccable. But he realised that something was needed beside
confrontation. The project had three objectives:

(a) to challenge members of the ruling group to see beyond
propaganda to the realities. One student who went to an all-
race conference organised in a township by Koinonia wrote in an
Afrikaans newspaper: "It only took one weekend to change me
from a conservative Afrikaner to an African. I shared your
ideas, your food, and even your beds. I will go back from here to
talk to my family, my friends, my political candidates..."

(b) to help the underdogs to keep a sense of common humanity
with their oppressors and a hope of converting them.

(c) to lay a foundation of relationships to strengthen the new
society at the end of the struggle.

In relation to the first point, Allan Boesak has written,

Genuine reconciliation does not occur between oppressor and
oppressed. It occurs between persons, persons who face each
other in their authentic, vulnerable and yet hopeful humanity.
And therefore liberation...is inevitably bound up with
reconciliation. And forgiveness[10].

And about the third, Akiki Bomera Mujaju says of Uganda:

Conditions of internal conflict...particularly those of a military
nature leave major scars on the bodies of the polity because
mutual animosity and bitterness may be long-lasting,
disrupting the process of developing stable, acceptable political
relations. Because the contestants are members of the same
country, [they] must learn to live together[11].

It would be difficult to argue that Koinonia and similar organisations
delayed the solution in South Africa, as the Kairos Document seemed
to fear. Any reconciliation project is a move against violence, because
it reduces the bitterness which leads to violence. But maximising
violence does not necessarily hasten the end of the conflict, let alone
create optimum conditions for peace. Koinonia contributed to the
struggle for justice by undermining the beliefs of the oppressors, but it
also offered them brotherhood and understanding. Such work is only
acceptable if it is honest. But its reward was that—without a
bloodbath—repression ended and the opportunity of freedom, peace
and justice arrived.

1   CIIR: *Challenge to the Churches (the Kairos document)* revised edn. 1986 p.9
2   Alan Boesak: *The Finger of God* (Maryknoll, USA: Orbis 1982) p.8
3   Dennis Sandole & Hugo van der Merwe: *Conflict Resolution: theory and practice* (Manchester: University Press 1995) p. 263
4   Donald Woods: *Biko* (Paddington Press, 1978) pp.64f.
5   Adam Curle: *Tools for Transformation* (Stroud: Hawthorn Press 1990) ch.11-12, esp. p.61
6   H.W. van der Merwe: *Pursuing Justice and Peace in South Africa* (Routledge, 1989) p.95
7   Richard Rosenthal, personal communication.
8   H.W. van der Merwe and Andries Odentaal in *Clinical Sociology Review* no.9, 1991
9   *Koinonia Newsletter* (1988) Vol.2 No.4
10 Boesak op.cit. p. 68
11 A.B.Mujaju (ed.): *Conflict Resolution in Uganda* (Oslo: IPRI, 1989) p.252

TEACHING PEACE IN A VIOLENT CONTEXT

Sezam

"Since wars begin in the minds of men," runs the UNESCO Charter, "it is in the minds of men that the defences of peace must be constructed." Yet only twenty years ago the idea of teaching children conflict handling skills was dismissed as eccentric. Today it is a strong movement in many countries, with international partnerships and a large literature. There is particular enthusiasm in some lands which have known recent violent conflict: Croatia, Romania, Rwanda, South Africa, Uganda; in Northern Ireland the government has incorporated "education for mutual understanding" into the National Curriculum. Here Sezam (whose name is derived from the magic words "Open, Sesame") describes its peace education work in postwar Bosnia.

The story of Sezam started with the International Medical Corps (IMC), a humanitarian organisation who came to our town of Zenica in Bosnia, in 1993. There were many international organisations who came to our town to help us. This group were concerned with problems of child mental health and devoted themselves to traumatised children in the collective centres around Zenica. In 1995 IMC decided to close down their programme, and some of us who were engaged in it decided to set up our own local group, as there were still many traumatised children in the Zenica area needing help. It was not an easy decision at the time, since the concept of a non-governmental organisation did not exist in our country before the war.

In the first three years, Sezam worked for traumatised children; but in the last two years we have changed our programme to peace education. So far 1300 children have passed through Sezam's activities. We work with children from six to twelve years old. Regarding the work with traumatised children, we organised structured activities where they could express themselves in a safe and positive environment. Through techniques like free writing, open discussion, storytelling and role-playing we give them an opportunity to talk about what they have been through, and how they feel about it. In peace education, our main goal was to help children to regain their self-confidence and improve their self-image which was tremendously damaged during the war. Through workshop activities we teach children to learn communication skills, a greater degree of tolerance and co-operation, leading to the ability to settle conflicts peacefully.

Sezam as an organisation had many ups and downs. But thankfully we have survived the past five years, thanks to the dedication of those who led the organisation and those who worked directly with the children. Sezam also had many friends all over the world, mainly in the United States, Switzerland, Ireland and Great Britain, who believed in what we do and gave us enormous support. At the beginning we had four people; now there are eleven in our team. Fuad, who joined in 1995 is our psychologist; at present he works as a professor in Sarajevo. Larissa, also from 1995, works on fundraising, proposal writing and publicising the organisation. She studies English language and literature. Venira, one of Sezam's founders, shares this work and co-ordinates the programme; she used to be a pre-school teacher. Those who work directly with children now include Naira, also a pre-school teacher, who joined in 1996; Aida, a former technologist, with us from 1995; Ivan, a primary school teacher, who joined in 1996; Emir, a student of the Pedagogical Academy, Benjamin, another teacher, and Valeria, a former dancing teacher, who came in 1997. Igda has looked after our finances since 1997, and Stanislav has been our driver and logistician from 1996.

The postwar context in Zenica

In the current year of 1999, three years after the end of the war, the problems already existing in our canton in Central Bosnia have deepened. The unresolved issues of unemployment and returnees, huge social differences caused by the war and the change of political system, the problem of demobilised soldiers who do not have any source of income and have been neglected by society, have led to an increased number of suicides compared to 1997/8. Local news media and medical centres report a growth in cancer and heart disease cases, due to the war and prolonged stress. Organised crime increases. There are more drug takers. There are severe housing problems. Following the political "solution", people are not satisfied with economic, health and social policies. Most people are dissatisfied with the Dayton Peace Accord and its results, because they expected something more.

The *Report on Violence against Women in Zenica* (Medika Infoteka, Zenica, April 1999) raises four issues, which are confirmed by our own enquiries:

1. *Reunited families.* Many reintegrated families in postwar Bosnia and Herzegovina are in a state of crisis. Respondents described a pattern rooted in the wartime circumstances where couples were separated; usually the man was in the army, away from home and the woman took on his family role in addition to her own. She had to provide for the family and ensure their protection and survival, nurture the children and manage the household. The war ended and the man came home. The family had to face the challenge of reintegrating its members.

2. *War trauma.* Respondents reported that men who had been in combat tended to express their emotions violently. They might find themselves unable to control anger, or show unusually intense reactions to normal situations.

3. *The postwar social situation.* This violence was interwoven with the stress of unemployment and inadequate financial resources. The resulting frustration causes constant conflict in the family. Inadequate funding of institutions causes a shortage of services, causing political and social tension. Another aspect of postwar society is the consequences of mass war migration; the loss of the community where a person had previously lived tore away an informal network of support among individuals which had provided security and advice in crisis situations. This was equally true of local people whose community left them, and for displaced people whose arrival changed the character of communities. People have moved from one cultural norm to another, causing huge stress in the family.

Such circumstances cause prolonged insecurity, weak motivation for work, changed values of life, increased aggressiveness and collective depression. The war changed values and distorted social relations, providing negative models for identification. The middle class has vanished; most people are struggling with irregular incomes, and some have no real income at all. During the war a few people became extremely rich through corruption, the black market, and the misuse of power.

In this difficult situation adolescent crime has increased. There are reports of more street gangs of young people, burglaries, prostitution, street violence and violence in schools. There are no organised cultural events in the town. Many young people and children spend their nights on the streets, gathering in front of the cafés and drinking cheap alcohol, smoking, and in many cases taking drugs, to escape the continuous conflict in their families, and the violence towards women and children at home.

There are still some "collective centres" in the gymnasiums of the schools, where displaced people have been living since 1992 in unbearable conditions. In some ways life is harder than during the war, because much of the work of the World Food Programme here has been closed down, and there is no more humanitarian aid.

The traumatic experiences of the war are still with us. Some families still do not know about missing members. There are also a lot of problems between those who stayed here during the war, those who are coming back from other countries where they went as refugees, and those who were displaced from other parts of Bosnia and settled in our town. These problems relate to legal regulations recently imposed by the international community: according to this law, anyone who is a refugee either here in Bosnia or in some other country should come back to his or her native home. These regulations are not applied in an equal way in the three parts of Bosnia and Herzegovina. For example, many people are forced to leave Western countries where they lived as refugees during the war; they come to Zenica rather than the town in Eastern Bosnia where their home is located. They tell us they would like to go home, but either they are afraid, because they experienced atrocities in that place during the war, or the local authorities there give them no help or encouragement to return.

Children in Zenica

All these problems affect the children we work with. They and their families have often been on the move for years. First they were forcibly displaced from their native homes. Then they had to adapt to life as refugees in a foreign country. Then the host country would not keep them; they had to return to Bosnia but could not go back to the place where they were born. For the third or fourth time in their lives they are living as refugees. In Sezam we have a girl who is a returnee from Hungary. She told us, "I hate it when other kids exclude me from their games—and it happens to me all the time!" We also noticed in Sezam that many children who are still living in the collective centres have difficulty taking part in the group, because they feel embarrassed.

Four years after the war, children still face so many problems. They are haunted by war memories. Here is part of the story of a boy of nine. He was three years old when this happened. He said:

> I was sitting in my grandfather's lap when soldiers came. They were shooting at my grandfather. They killed him. They threw me away into a bush. Then they left. I was left on my own, wandering through the wood. Some time later some people found me and helped me to find my parents.

Here is the story of an eleven year old girl.

> When I was with my grandparents in the summer holidays, a drunken neighbour threw a bomb into our house. I was so scared. Since then I'm always nervous. I was five. I was scared to death. I thought I was going to die. Even now I'm scared to go to the toilet alone.

We have chosen one more story, from a twelve year old boy who is a refugee from Banja Luka, a town in the Serbian part of our country. He has been living with his parents and siblings in one of the collective centres in Zenica. While at home he witnessed the killing of his grandfather, and in 1998, his father was murdered in the collective centre. In one session the boy said:

> I was expelled from home, and I wandered with my family all through Bosnia looking for just a small piece of my prewar life. There was shelling, and I moved from one shelter to another. I was a little boy, that's why I was very scared.

In one of his individual sessions with us, we found out they were going to move from the collective centre to an apartment in a suburb of the town. Afterwards the boy said: "I was far away from my home, and I don't have the right conditions for living. But it's useless to look for my home."

Sezam's peace education work

At first, during the war, we chose children so as to give them a secure environment to share their experiences of war atrocities and displacement with us, where they could feel safe because they had nowhere else to do this. Later on when the Dayton Peace Agreement officially stopped the war, we knew that Bosnian society still had numerous problems which had not been solved; this motivated us to develop our programme.

Working with the children and their traumas, our team began to feel we were all prisoners of these war memories. We felt exhausted—and perhaps the children did too. We wanted to change this. We wanted to find the strength to look forwards, for ourselves and for the children. In the general collapse and loss of values, we decided that the children are our future. We wanted to give them so much strength that we could believe in them as the real future of our country. In fact we wanted to change the future to one of peace.

We know from our work that one of the most frequent results of war trauma in children is loss of confidence, in oneself, one's abilities, and the people around one. This leads to poor and distorted communication to other children, in the family and in school. So peace education was a natural continuation of our work on trauma issues. We did not want to deny, hide or forget what had happened to each of us. But our work had shown us how dreadful and horrifying life could become for children; so we wanted to do something to prevent it happening again, and give our children the chance to live in a more peaceful environment. We, who had experienced the war, wanted to create a new strength which would expand and give our children a positive energy, so that in ten years they would be self-confident young women and men, able to learn, able to search, willing to love others rather than hating them. We wanted them to feel satisfied with themselves.

Peace education, working on co-operation skills, good communication, and respect for oneself and others, ensures peace within ourselves and in our environment. We enhance our positive thinking. Conflict becomes a problem which affects both sides, interfering with the fulfilment of both sides' wishes and needs. We cannot avoid conflict—but we can solve it without aggression. Peace education supports healthy communication and gives different mechanisms for conflict solutions. It is essential to the development of a healthy democratic society. It is particularly important after war. We did not want old mistakes to be repeated. There are so many tensions within our society, which is not very open to change; changes happen slowly, with difficulty. It is not easy to alter the ideas of the adult world. This was the biggest reason which persuaded us to work with children.

In our programme we give children different models of communication and values to what they find in our present society. Sezam also gives them the chance to learn new models for conflict resolution. We teach them to think about themselves and about other people in a new way, understanding the relationship between them. The learning is through games, exercises, circle time, storytelling, problem solving together, discussions, and adult-child friendships. During the process the children grow in confidence in themselves and other people. For instance we have an activity called "Supportive Game" in which they have blank sheets of paper stuck to their backs, on which others write positive thoughts and feelings about them. This encourages positive thinking about others, a more positive self-image, and a sense of group support.

The children, of course, spend most of their time in school. We realised that the relationship between teacher and child in our society is based on authority, which invites the misuse of power. This causes a lot of problems. We actually want to change that relationship between the teacher and the children, and to create one in which teachers respect the needs of each child—while the child respects the needs of the teacher. We believe that such a relationship helps the children to become responsible individuals, which we find very important.

Our programme is based on eight cycles, which have different themes: "Through games to ourselves", "Through games to other people", "We are all different", "Competition and co-operation", "Co-operation and tolerance". "Conflict", "Conflict resolution" and "Be careful with anger". These themes and cycles are taken from the book *Budimo Prijatelji (Let's be Friends)* produced by the group Mali Korak (Small Step) in Croatia, and written by Maja Uzelac, Aida Bagic and Ladislav Bognar.

Our children are divided into groups. Each group consists of ten to fifteen children led by one male and one female group facilitator. Each group session has three parts, starting with an introductory game to relax and encourage communication. Activities follow on the main topic (from one of the cycles already mentioned); this is followed by a final game to leave the children with a feeling of pleasure at belonging to the group.

In our 1998 programme we also included a group of teachers, from the school where we work with the children. We also made radio programmes to spread the idea that peace skills can be learnt. We think that our peace education in Sezam helps the children, their families, their school, and our whole society.

Our future plans

We want to spread these benefits to a new group of twenty five teenagers; we hope they will one day become leaders of groups of younger children. We want to form a new teachers' group from different schools, as the teacher is such an important person in the life of the child.   They spend so much time with children that they could be the best messengers of the philosophy with which we work.   We want to develop our radio programme, and to be more visible in all the public media.   We want to expand our relations with other peace organisations in former Yugoslavia.   We have had a successful contact with the Centre for Peace Studies in Zagreb; but we met other groups at conference sometimes which we have not followed up, such as Most (Bridge) in Belgrade, and the Youth Organisation in Macedonia.   We have mostly co-operated with groups in our own part of Bosnia (the Federation of Bosnia-Herzegovina), but recently we have noticed that it is now easier to communicate with groups in the other part, Republika Srpska, which was very difficult before.   This is real progress.   We very often feel lonely in our work, so we would like all the organisations who work for a peaceful future to get together and strive for greater recognition for us all.

Regarding our dream to have a wider effect on Bosnia, Sezam would like to create a much larger group of people committed to our philosophy—a larger group of beneficiaries perhaps, but above all a change so that our schools in Bosnia are places where children are not afraid to go.   We would like the ideas and activities we share with our children to become a part of normal school life.   We dream of teachers who are willing to be open and accepting, who will share these ideals and methods with the children.

The war changed us all, but each person was affected in a different way.   But our common conclusion was how cruel, horrifying and brutal war is.   Sezam's work is the result of war.   We are witnesses to thousands of lives which have been interrupted or broken.   Families were destroyed or broken up.   Their members sometime died or disappeared.   Many people lived in the concentration camps or as refugees. Because of all these altered lives, because the way our society divided and collapsed, and because of the changes in ourselves, we can clearly see the new development Bosnia needs.

At present adult society is composed of people who were never given the chance to experience a programme such as ours.   In most cases school did not teach them to be responsible for themselves and use a critical intelligence—only to listen and obey.   We do not want the future of Bosnia to stand on that basis.   In fact we find it hard to work with such people and teach them peaceful approaches to problems, though we are sometimes successful.   In contrast, we see children as the purest human beings, with whom we have a chance to improve the future of Bosnia.

WORKING FOR POLITICAL CHANGE

Michael Bartlet

Many people are sceptical of the value of lobbying their Members of Parliament. But MPs are thinking people, and need to be sensitive to the concerns of their constituents. Michael Bartlet, Parliamentary Liaison Secretary for the Society of Friends, urges us to persevere with such contacts, and suggests how to be most effective.[1]

The nineteenth-century Quaker MP, John Bright, clearly expressed his motivation: "the moral law is intended not for individual life only, but for the life and practice of states in their dealings with one another." He withdrew his support from the government in 1882 over the bombing of Alexandria but this was in the context of forty years' political loyalty and in carefully calibrated terms: 'I think that in the present case there has been a manifest violation of international law and the moral law and therefore it is impossible for me to give my support to it.'

Jim Challis, a former civil servant, in his involvement in planning and setting up the post of parliamentary liaison secretary for the Religious Society of Friends (or Quakers) saw its role as "expressing our spiritual insights in the context of political discussion". I find it hard to give reasons for Quakers' involvement in politics except to turn the question around and wonder how anyone who cares about the world can not be involved in politics. The Society of Friends has a long tradition of active witness and involvement in national and international affairs.

Political expression of our values derives from the Quaker process of corporate discernment and decision making. Those of us who work centrally in Britain Yearly Meeting must be committed to this. Any expression of policy has to be rooted in consultation, discussing concerns nationally and making the link between local and national work. The parliamentary liaison secretary works both by informing Friends of what is happening politically and also in a more active role of advocacy, pursuing concerns politically. These two aspects of my work are two sides of the same coin. One of the most challenging injunctions in the gospel is to "be as innocent as doves and wise as serpents". However far we fall short, that saying contains a realism which understands the ways of the world without being overwhelmed by them. We need to recognise both principles if we are to be effective and effective in the right cause.

Any influence that Quakers have nationally depends on the strength and quality of local contacts. Our countrywide network of parliamentary links is the blood and lymph of any political influence that we have. So here are a few guidelines on sharing your concerns with your MPs.

The first golden rule to remember is we have no power except that which we share and derive from consent. All we can seek to do is to nudge. When we fail to recognise this and so misperceive the extent of our national authority—when we assume that the government is just waiting to listen to what the Quakers have to say—we usually miscommunicate. If we are seeking to change opinions we have to give people reasons. We have to root our concerns in experience and truth. Experience here is best when real and immediate. As Basil Hume put it, "Sincerity is the heart of oratory." There is no substitute for clearly communicated expertise. So clearly someone who has had experience of prisons can best speak of the need for penal reform, and someone who has had experience of the army can best talk of the danger of the recruitment of under-eighteen-year-olds into the armed forces.

To achieve change we have to appeal to both enlightened self-interest and altruism. To give one practical example here—telling an MP with a slim majority, in an area where jobs are dependent on arms manufacturing, that we think the arms trade is morally wrong is going to be less effective than advocating alternative employment and proposing a technology applications agency which would help to find civilian uses for military technology. We have nothing to fear from appropriately directed self-interest. William Temple (a bishop and a socialist) described politics as "the art of so ordering society that self-interest prompts what justice requires". Any society that fails to take account of self-interest will be inherently unstable. As a friend and colleague of mine put it, "I would be rather suspicious of someone who thought they did things only for the highest motives: they would probably lack self-knowledge."

A second key to success is to make common cause. Find out your MP's interests, do some research, give them all the information they need and allow them to make up their mind. There is no better argument than the facts. Are we really respecting the conscience of another if we tell them what they ought to think? The best form of advocacy is almost always the gentlest. The most effective tone is perhaps a quiet confidence, remembering that governments need to be lobbied. They need input from organisations in order both to test the waters and to fine-tune policies.

After the building of the Berlin Wall, American Quakers appointed a Quaker International Affairs Representative (QIAR) to the two Germanies, to try to develop viable personal relationships with people in and outside government, study the situation and report on it, and try to exercise a modest influence towards a peaceful solution of the very real conflicts of interest and ideology. One important issue was the human hardships caused by the Wall. "It was basic to this relationship that the officials perceive the QIAR as truly friendly, not 'captured' by the propaganda of the other side, not a party to the Cold War. Another important aspect of the situation was that the QIAR was quite willing to acknowledge or even assert what he thought to be unfortunate actions on the other side as well. ...The officials— whether in West or East Berlin (East Berlin was the capital of the GDR) or in the American Embassy or the FRG government in Bonn—were highly interested in the assessment of an independent observer who they believed spoke as a friend rather than an antagonist. One should add that it was necessary they should perceive that the QIAR had 'done his homework' and was highly knowledgeable on the issues discussed."[2]

Thirdly, suit your arguments to your person. To take the example of crime: simply saying we ought to be more compassionate to criminals isn't going to get us anywhere if we are talking to an MP in a constituency where concern over crime and its effects is the number one issue. We might have more chance of success by looking at re-offending rates, emphasising the cost and ineffectiveness of an undue reliance on prison, and making proposals for what a better trained and funded probation service might look like. The crucial point still is to appeal to, and in the deepest sense recognise and respect, the person that you are speaking to.

So if your burning interest is disarmament and you have a Conservative MP, far better than speaking of the evils of imperialism might be to talk with genuine respect about the achievements of previous governments in bloodlessly giving up empire. To recognise the skill of Lord Carrington in mediating over the independence of Zimbabwe and then to show how nuclear disarmament could be the most powerful and patriotic lead that Britain could give—not giving up power but gaining influence through courageous diplomatic initiative—

might be a more appropriate way of approaching the issue than bold statements from an imaginary moral high ground.

Remember that most MPs have at best a modest influence on events. But if we have a chance to speak to a Minister, or decide to write, we should bear in mind what Giandomenico Pico, a former Assistant Secretary General at the United Nations has said, "Too rarely we consider that it may be quite easy to write a piece criticising a foreign policy line—if we are not responsible for what happens the day after".

A fourth guideline is to look to solutions rather than emphasise problems. This may be harder but it is more useful. With a few exceptions, an MP will probably be more aware of most problems in the constituency than you are. What you can do is to propose the solutions. For example, in the case of homelessness, the kind of programmes that are going to be most effective in combating it are practical and to the point, like the Quaker Homeless Action's rent guarantee scheme. We all know that there are young people who cannot afford to get into rented property because they can't afford the deposit. Working to provide a guarantee and then speaking with authority from that perspective will carry more weight than simply expounding the problem.

This is as true internationally as at home. Solutions are more attractive than stark presentations of facts. Andrew Clark (former General Secretary of Quaker Peace & Service) describes diplomacy as the art of giving people ladders to climb down. We all need this from time to time, not least politicians. Informed advocacy in favour of a just and compassionate common European foreign policy may have more effect than bald condemnation of Britain's use of sanctions and bombing of Iraq or Serbia.

For example, the Quaker United Nations Office in Geneva has been working to end the use of children as soldiers[3].   They began collecting and analysing information and then consulting with governments and international organisations concerned with the welfare of children.   Despite the obvious humanitarian issue, with perhaps 30,000 children currently fighting in wars, many countries were slow to support the UN Conventions which could work to end the practice.

While the Geneva Office focuses primarily on the international dimension, the issue has important ramifications in the United Kingdom.   The UK government currently has over 6000 sixteen and seventeen year olds in the armed forces—and since 1982 a total of ninety two UK service personnel who were aged 16 or 17 have died while in the armed services. While the UK government's campaign against the coercion of young people into armies is welcome, its own practice undermines its efforts.

Quakers were able to raise the parliamentary profile of this issue by drafting Parliamentary Questions and Early Day Motions (a sort of parliamentary petition). They got a supportive MP to table the following Motion: That this House welcomes the announcement of the Under-Secretary of Peacekeeping at the United Nations that under-18 year olds will not be included in UN peacekeeping missions; notes with regret that over 6000 young people aged 16 and 17 are in the United Kingdom armed forces; urges Her Majesty's Government further to work internationally for an optional Protocol to the UN Convention on the Rights of the Child enjoining all countries to ensure that no one under the age of 18 bears arms; and notes that the current practice of recruiting minors into the armed forces undermines the Government's campaign against the coercion of young people into the armed forces of those countries engaged in armed conflict. Forty four MPs currently support this Motion.

An effective campaign will approach an issue from several angles. So in addition to raising the issue from the perspective of the UN Convention on the Rights of the Child, the Quaker Office in Geneva consulted with governments, trades unions, employers and child labour NGOs and pressed with some success for "child soldiering" to be included in the new International Labour Organisation Convention on the Worst Forms of Child Labour. (Early Day Motions in our own parliament are supporting this.) In Parliament the issue can also be raised from the perspective of European Law, where there is a conflict between the 1994 Council Directive "on the protection of young people at work" and the practice of having minors in the armed forces. It has also been possible to include submissions on the issue to the Defence Select Committee and it is hoped to table a Ten-minute-rule Bill in the next session of Parliament. There has always been a strong link in democracies between bearing arms and the right to vote. Perhaps the most powerful point that can be made is the injustice of allowing people to fight for an army over which they have no political control.

An issue such as Kossovo raises deeply complex problems. While it is vital that a whole range of opinions are heard, once the bombs have started falling it is probably too late to do much. Legislation to allow the UK to ratify the Statute of the International Criminal Court may go some way to helping provide the building blocks of an international rule of law. Beyond that, if we are to prevent future Kosovos we should press our government to place conflict prevention at the heart of the work of the UN, recognising the financial implications. In Yugoslavia there was plenty of information on the likelihood of conflict since before the death of Marshall Tito. In Rwanda threats to the Tutsi minority were well known before violence exploded. What is needed is to strengthen and formalise the channels of information, and to ensure that when warning signals are received they appear on the agenda of the Security Council.

Fifthly and crucially, find out who your allies are. On freedom of information, for example, work with the Freedom of Information Campaign. On the problems of indebtedness go both for information and as local allies to the World Development Movement and Jubilee 2000. In our efforts to end war, there are many connections to be made with human rights advocates (such as Amnesty International) and opponents of the arms trade (Campaign Against the Arms Trade). Recognise the global reach of the problem (United Nations Association, UNESCO's work to develop "a culture of peace", and the World Council of Churches' Programme to Overcome Violence) as well as its environmental implications (Greenpeace). Remember, too, the importance of working with other churches and other faiths. The way that Islam is sometimes portrayed in the public media is a source of international tension (for instance during the war in Bosnia); are there local opportunities to reduce misperceptions?

Finally, work as a local group. There is all the difference between approaching an MP as an individual and as an organisation. One of the most creative ideas that some Quaker meetings have been involved with is asking an MP to come and meet with them as a meeting. This establishes a natural constituency link and helps inform the MP about local concerns. Such an encounter works on several levels. Firstly it gives the MP the opportunity to understand what we as Quakers are about. It is a way of showing that we are concerned with them as individuals and not as slot machines for political manipulation. You may even be able to ground your meeting in worship. The silence and worshipful reflection are as valuable as your views. You can make the connection between your faith and your work.

Efforts at an institutional level are not enough. Adam Curle points out, "the task for would-be peace-makers must be on two levels. They must dig out the roots of unpeacefulness within themselves: the blindness, the illusory sense of 'I', the cravings and antipathies and guilts. Without this effort, however partially successful, they can never hope to have any real effect on others."4

Perhaps at the heart of all work with MPs is the need to remember that, as God is in us, He or She is as surely in those with whom we meet and speak. Or to put it in another way—we all share a common humanity. Universal human rights in the twentieth century is the secular counterpart of the seventeenth-century insight that there is that of God in everyone. That presence is no less true of those who feel uncomfortable about using the language of God. The testimony to equality is not a uniquely Quaker concept. One of the most poignant moments in the gospel is when Christ turns to the disciples and expresses that equality: "I no longer call you servants but friends for I have revealed to you all that I know."

At the heart of real peacemaking is forgiveness. Diana Lampen recounts from her experience in Northern Ireland how a friend of hers, an ex-terrorist, was talking to Mary whose husband (unknown to him) had been killed years before by his former organisation. He was dangerously ill, and he told Mary about his involvement in violence. Then he asked her story, and discovered with a shock that he could have been her husband's killer. Finding from the details that it could not have been him, he said, "Thank God I didn't kill him." Mary's response was, "I wish it had been you so I could show you that I forgive you." It is only through such forgiveness, which we all need to receive and to give, that we can create the relationships from which we can build more peaceful communities.

Just like us, anyone we meet will respond most effectively to support, empathy, and encouragement when we feel that they can do something positive. Courtesy (hard as it may be) is the hallmark of good communication. Our relationship with an MP is one of constituent to representative; clear and balanced opinions courteously voiced should never be a problem but part of the support we can give to enable them to represent the views of their constituents in the forum to which they have been elected.

What George Herbert wrote three hundred years ago amid the turbulence of the English revolution is as true today as it was then:

Be calm in arguing; for fierceness makes
Error a fault, and truth discourtesy.
Why should I feel another man's mistake
More than his sickness or his poverty?
In love I should; but anger is not love,
Nor wisdom neither; therefore gently move.

References

1   An earlier version of this paper appeared in *Quaker Monthly*, May 1999.
2   Roland Warren in *Quaker Experiences of Political Mediation*   (QPS, 1990.)
3   See articles by Rachel Brett in *The Friend*, 6.8.1999 and 10.9.1999
4   Adam Curle: *Tools for Transformation*   (Hawthorn Press, 1990)

WHAT CAN I DO? THE PLACE OF DIRECT ACTION AS RESISTANCE

Helen Steven

We can feel powerless when our government carries out violent policies of which we disapprove. Helen Steven, a nonviolent campaigner for many years, examines the tacit assent which governments rely on, and shows how it can be challenged.

The twentieth century has witnessed such a litany of atrocities from Belsen to Hiroshima, My Lai to Rwanda that it has come to be known as "the bloody century". Already we are predicting a 21st Century of vicious ethnic conflict, intolerable pressure of a growing population on decreasing natural resources, and the rise of ruthless dictators. It is a grim picture and one before which it is so easy to despair and feel totally powerless. As Professor Gene Sharp of Harvard University states;

> We have to a large degree lost the confidence, and even the hope, that we can solve our most serious domestic and international problems. This loss alone must be placed high on the list of the tragedies of the 20th Century.[1]

But with the founding of the U.N. Charter to "save succeeding generations from the scourge of war", and the launch of the year 2000 as the year of Nonviolence, initiating the Decade for a Culture of Peace we can also see the expression of a deep human longing to see nonviolence work.

It becomes ever more urgent then as we move into the next century that we find adequate nonviolent responses to the agonising dilemma of ruthless dictators, oppressive regimes, and increasing terror and suffering. When faced with the haggard faces of terrified refugees, violated women, brutalised children, the response of caring humanity must be to take action, to become engaged, to do something. But so often the only choice open to us seems to be the violent option; to bring in the bombers, to mount a military invasion, to execute, assassinate, control. And in so acting the seeds of the next oppressive regime and violent conflict are already sown and the cycle of violence continues.

107

Take, for example, the NATO bombing of Kosovo. As the bombing progressed week after week it became increasingly obvious that it was having grave repercussions on the whole democratic structure of the Balkans, and that the potential for conflict and destabilisation would spread far beyond the borders of Serbia and Kosovo. The *Statement of Concerned Serbian Citizens*, signed by many of the leading politicians, journalists and academics in Serbia, including the president of the Helsinki Citizens Assembly, describes how the NATO bombing was causing major destabilisation in the whole Balkan region, how opposition parties were being forced underground, and how they had serious fears for the future of any kind of democratic government in the future[2]. Many commentators at the time predicted widespread conflict spilling over the borders as the pressure from refugees grew, and subsequent events have shown how revenge killings erupted whenever the bombing stopped. Few people believe that the Balkans are enjoying any measure of long-term peace as a result of NATO intervention.

The onus remains upon those of us who work for a peaceful world to offer some credible alternatives. This chapter is written in the firm personal belief that "World peace will come through the will of ordinary people like ourselves" and that committed nonviolent action can and does create the change necessary to transform violence. It is not giving blueprints or answers, but a few pointers and examples of the kind of simple things that ordinary people can do, which added together form strong opposition to oppression at all levels.

> For those of us who still believe that human dignity, creativity, justice and freedom are important, the nonviolent technique of struggle may provide one of our last hopes for effective reversal of the current directions toward dehumanisation, regimentation, manipulation, and the dominance of political structures of violence and tyranny.[3]   (Gene Sharp)

It might be helpful to consider briefly how nonviolence actually works. Some of us who remember the anti-nuclear movements of the '70's and '80's may be familiar with "George Lakey's Spiral" showing the development of a movement from the point at which an individual sees an issue as important, through the stages of communication and organisation of a movement, to the point of mass demonstrations, huge public events, to the eventual transformation of society—not that any movement is ever as neat and tidy as that! In his analysis George Lakey talks of the "propaganda of the deed", and it is this vitally transformative action, often of a symbolic nature, that is at the heart of nonviolent action for change. Raising public awareness of an issue is crucial, but it should be done in such a way that people themselves are changed. In this way the actions of ordinary people draw attention to oppression and injustice; to quote Martin Luther King, "Nonviolence exposes the latent violence of society"[4], and far more than that, by the methods of nonviolence attitudes are changed as well. To quote King again "We will match your capacity to inflict suffering with our capacity to endure suffering. We will meet your physical force with soul force. We will not hate you, but we cannot in good conscience obey your unjust laws....and in winning our freedom we will win you in the process."

An essential element of nonviolent social change is the withdrawal of consent. Structures of society, even the most tyrannical, are held in place by general acceptance. The little booklet entitled *People Power* shows a diagram of "The Ruler" held in place by an edifice of building blocks. These are such societal factors as control of knowledge, control of resources, acceptance of an ideology, psychological factors, customary norms and habits, and ultimately the  sanction of force. Remove consent, challenge and defy the sanctions that uphold the system, and the structure falls.

This may sound facile and glib in the face of ruthless and brutal oppression, but studies have shown that even Eichman's programme of genocide could have been resisted at many stages. Hannah Arendt in her book *Eichman in Jerusalem* points to the ease with which the whole climate of fear enabled the Nazi administration to carry out genocide without fear of intervention or reprisals.

> Clearly it was not the administrative apparatus that these first operations were supposed to test. The objective seems to have been a test of general political conditions whether Jews could be made to walk to their doom ....what the reaction of their neighbours would be .....how foreign governments would react when presented with thousands of Jewish refugees. As far as the Nazis could see, everything turned out very satisfactorily[5].

Time and again we hear of nonviolent resistance movements which have failed because of lack of response from outside—the White Rose in Nazi Germany, Rugova in Kosovo, the early stages of anti-apartheid.

The problem is that so often we are presented with an apparently clear choice: use military intervention or do nothing—"Let Bosnia/Kosovo/East Timor burn". The nonviolent choice is never between doing violence and doing nothing. Nonviolence is about finding the creative alternative and always standing up against evil and oppression. A recent example shows how the creative nonviolent response was able to turn a violent situation around. In response to the brutal rampages of the anti-independence militias in East Timor, the U.N. had ordered a complete withdrawal of their unarmed personnel in Dili, thus leaving at least 1000 refugees at the mercy of the militia. 80 U.N. personnel refused to go, risking their lives but providing time for the international community to respond.

And resistance to oppression cannot begin too soon. There must be a refusal to accept or condone humiliation or any denial of human rights at its very first appearance. Elias Chacour, a Palestinian writer, once said "The holocaust began when the first person was able to say 'dirty Jew' and get away with it."[6] The longer such resistance is postponed or avoided, the harder and the costlier such resistance will be—to the point where it does seem as if resorting to violence is the only way to halt oppression.

Challenging the control of knowledge

Perhaps the place to start is by becoming better informed ourselves, then raising awareness of the issues in others around us in a real effort to seek the truth. This enables us to break down the barriers to communication, break through the stereotypes. Then we have to attempt to persuade by our actions in such a way that we are reaching out to the humanity of the other, so that minds can actually change. And finally we may have to go the length of putting our bodies on the line to prevent violence from happening.

At all of these levels there are so many things that each of us, no matter how hampered or diffident we might be, can do. We are not all required to stand alone in front of the tanks (thank goodness), but we must discover what we are capable of. A woman joined our newly-formed C.N.D. group in Stirling in the early '80's. Knowing that she was dying of cancer she explained that she couldn't attend meetings or go on demonstrations, but she wrote letters for the group until the week that she died.

A crucial element in the structures of oppression is the control of knowledge, so we have a duty to be accurately informed. Yet how often have we rushed to a map of the world trying to find the country which is currently in the news. Of course we are bombarded with all kinds of news and information and part of the difficulty is sifting out the truth from the hype. Reporters like John Pilger have been telling us for many years about the Indonesian government's oppression of East Timor, so it should have come to us as no surprise when violence broke out. Sometimes they are straws in the wind, but when Amnesty International reports recurring human rights abuses we would do well to take note. Nowadays the internet provides information that can escape censorship and control and is international in its source. We have an obligation to try to discern the truth beyond the media stories. Perhaps one of the simplest actions we can take is to have a map of the world on the kitchen wall!

The next stage of course is alerting other people; disseminating the information and courageous whistleblowing. Mordechai Vanunu has spent the last thirteen years in prison in Israel (eleven and a half of them in solitary confinement) for making public the information on the development of Israel's nuclear weapon capability. We are fortunate in the U.K. that we have freedom of speech and a free press, and certainly we do not run the risk of torture and disappearance for publishing, but we must be conscious of the limitations of the media and be prepared to find alternative ways of communicating. Newsletters like Peace News, Amnesty, and C.A.A.T. News all need our support. And sometimes we have to create our own media. During the Kosovo crisis the Centre for Nonviolence where I work had so many people asking us for advice and information that we logged onto one of the internet information links and then produced and distributed a weekly digest of information.

An information success story was the production of the Gulfwatch Papers.[7] A week before the hostilities broke out in the Gulf, a group of us were sitting round the fire in the library of Peace House sharing our despair and helplessness. I expressed my feeling of sadness as a historian that any semblance of truth was about to be lost in a tide of war propaganda. We then shared what skills we had—these ranged from computer expertise to first hand experience of the Middle East, to a willingness to lick stamps and stuff envelopes. And so the Gulfwatch Papers were born—an alternative analysis of the situation in the Gulf which came out as one sheet of A4 every day of the war and was distributed to well over 7,000 people using e-mail and ordinary post. Many people later told me it was their lifeline of hope through these dark days. It was later published by the Edinburgh Review and has been lodged in the Imperial War Museum as an archive.

Regimes depend for their power on control of resources, both material and financial. This is where the power of the consumer can be so effective. From the sailing of medical supplies to Hanoi at the height of the Vietnam war to the small group of people who are repeatedly and courageously breaking the sanctions on Iraq, there have always been people willing to defy crippling blockades of supplies. From Nestle products to GM foods we are now well aware of the power of boycott. During the time of the French nuclear tests, I was on a flight between Edinburgh and Brussels. The air hostess asked if I would like red or white wine, and when I asked if it was French she replied: "Oh no madam, there's been far too much protest for our airline to stock French wine."

The banking system is particularly sensitive to the fluctuations of world affairs. At the time of the apartheid regime in South Africa students in particular used a variety of creative ways of putting pressure on Barclays Bank to withhold its support for the regime. One tactic was for students up and down the country to queue up at the check-outs making lengthy requests about the withdrawal of their accounts, to the point where banks came to a standstill. There is a possibly apocryphal tale that, as the Jacobite army was approaching Derby in 1746, London was thrown into a panic and there was a run on the Bank of England as people rushed to withdraw their savings. Realising that the crisis might pass soon, the Bank heated the coins red-hot so that customers couldn't pick them up quickly! Perhaps Barclays should have taken note.

Without our taxes, of course, governments would be financially crippled. In Scotland over 50% of the people refused to pay the Poll Tax, which so many considered an unjust burden on the poor, and thus played a direct part in bringing down the Conservative government. I am puzzled to know why more people who are conscientious objectors don't question the Inland Revenue about the payment of the 12% of their taxes that is spent on defence.

One of the most vital aspects of attempting to discern the truth is to seek the root causes of the conflict. In 1972 I was working with a Quaker project in Vietnam. My initial involvement arose out of a somewhat naive altruistic desire to "do something" about the war. Working in orphanages we may have done a little bit to alleviate suffering, although nothing more than the Vietnamese could do, but the main lesson I learned was that the best way of helping the Vietnamese people was to go back home and tackle the real causes of their suffering by campaigning to end the war. This search for the root causes involves engaging with the complexities of the military industrial nexus, and exposing them in ways that bring clarity. During the Gulf War, for example, a German highlighted the connection with western dependence on oil resources by chaining his Volkswagen out on his own front lawn with a huge placard saying "The real cause of the war". Dramatic and symbolic changes of lifestyle can also help to highlight the causes of oppression and focus on our own or our government's part in oppressive regimes. Placing the blame where it really lies saves us from an easy complacency.

The Quaker John Woolman said; "May we look upon our treasures, the furniture of our houses, and our garments, and try whether the seeds of war have nourishment in these our possessions."[8]

Ideological and psychological control of people's minds and opinions is another of the building blocks of oppression, often whipped up and exaggerated by a controlled media. The speed with which exaggerated enemy images and demonisation can occur is particularly alarming. Against a background of "Saddam the Rat", "Hang Saddam Long and Slow" I had the temerity to suggest to the Military Staff College at Camberley that we should attempt to listen to the Iraqi side of the story. My audience actually hissed! There is such a huge task of listening and creating safe spaces where such listening can happen. There is a delicate balance between retelling history to enable better understanding and dwelling on past bitterness to foster hatred. But only when history is listened to, grievances acknowledged, and past hurts shared, can memory become a healing and reconciling process. There is much we can do to encourage real listening.

There are many examples of creative work which challenge our stereotypes. During the Cold War a huge poster which bore the slogan "The Russians Are Coming" showed a beautiful picture of a Bolshoi ballerina. At the end of the Gulf War a week was held in the Abbey on Iona for Jews, Christians and Muslims to share their experiences of living in Britain during the war. Recently a small group came together in the Nonviolence Centre in Dunblane simply to share their confusion and bewilderment about the war in Kosovo, and at the end of October a delegation is going from Scotland to Bosnia to visit joint Christian-Muslim reconciliation projects in Sarajevo and Tuzla. It requires a constant seeking for "that of God" in the other and (no matter how hard it seems) a refusal ever to let other human beings be demeaned or humiliated.

Direct Action

George Lakey's "propaganda of the deed" is a vital stage in any campaign, and most of us are familiar with this aspect of symbolic direct action. The task is to expose tyranny and corruption and the part we play in it and to offer ways out. It is here that creative nonviolence takes off into a whole range of funny, solemn, eye-catching events. We all have our stories, and they all play their part in taking away the mystique of fear or habitual unquestioning obedience of authority.

Memories of carrying a coffin draped in a Nicaraguan flag to protest U.S. aid to the Contras. We walked the length of Princes Street in Edinburgh from the West End to the U.S. Consulate—all done at funeral pace, which of course held up all the traffic in Edinburgh city centre, as no-one likes to run over pall-bearers! Or the time in the U.S.A. when a group of us occupied a Senator's office, sitting in total silence around the walls while the secretaries stepped over and around us. There are many imaginative ways in which ordinary folk by simple symbolic action can draw attention to injustice. Withholding our taxes, demonstrating on the streets, holding silent vigils, blockade running, boycotts, the list is endless, and often more effective than we realise.

Such actions seem so trivial and almost self-congratulatory when carried out in a context in which peaceful protest is allowed, but this must not detract from the fact that it is by such small seemingly insignificant actions that public opinion is alerted and informed to the point where governments can be forced to take action. Some of the most inspiring examples of small simple actions have taken place in a context of extreme oppression, to notable effect. We might say that in this country wearing a badge is one of the easiest forms of protest, but set in a different context it suddenly becomes an act of defiance. In the now famous occasion when the Nazis decreed that all Jews in Denmark must wear the yellow star, the King of Denmark wore a star, thus by a very simple courageous act nullifying the oppressive orders. During the '80's in Eastern Europe, when protesters were forbidden by the government from wearing the "swords into ploughshares" logo, they simply cut a hole in their sleeves where the badge might have been, thus avoiding arrest, as no-one can be arrested for having torn clothes! Members of the Norwegian Resistance during World War II wore paper clips in their lapel to show their allegiance. Such simple but effective actions.

I am a member of a small nonviolent direct action group in Scotland, and some years ago we were all horrified by a T.V. programme which showed the export of electric shock batons from a factory in Glasgow to Saudi Arabia where they were being used for torture. We determined to use symbolic action to expose this trade to the local people of Glasgow as part of a campaign to bring the owner of the company to justice. Members of our group, using a cardboard template, spray-painted "bloody" footprints going from the gates of the factory down to the traffic lights on the main street. When we came to court we had a sympathetic hearing and were given an unconditional discharge. Amnesty International and C.A.A.T. raised the matter through the courts and eventually the owner was brought to trial and found guilty of the illegal export of arms. Just one small victory.

It is such actions, however, which create the climate of opinion in which change can happen. Twenty years of Chile solidarity concerts, Amnesty International letter-writing campaigns, public meetings with refugees, films, books, talks and lectures all played their part in making the name of Pinochet so well known that when it came to the point of government decisions on extradition, there was already a huge groundswell of informed public opinion.

> The concept of acceptable change can offer no panaceas, no easy path, no guaranteed safety, no assurances of success in every respect and on each occasion. However the possibility exists that we can deliberately contribute to the development of a new stage of human history. We can resolve the acute problems with which we have been confronted for so long. We can be on the verge of a new departure of human capacities, which we can develop if we wish, in order that people can regain, or perhaps for many achieve for the first time, the capacity to control their own destinies.[9]
> (Gene Sharp)

Direct action, of course goes far beyond this even to the point of putting one's life on the line. The world was shocked into awareness of the horrors of the Vietnam war when Buddhist monks burned themselves to death, and the callous response of the Saigon government to such sacrifices led in part to its downfall. Some years ago I visited Wenceslas Square and saw the place where the Czech student dissident, Jan Pallach, had burned himself to death. There is a small parapet around the spot about half a metre high, and when I touched it I realised that it was made of wax from the thousands of candles burned in his memory ever since his death. Surely a most telling and moving focal point of resistance. The picture of the Chinese student confronting the line of tanks in Tiananmen Square has become one of the classic images of nonviolent resistance.

As I write this chapter, U.N. troops are attempting to restore order in East Timor. Until a few years ago very few people knew where East Timor was, let alone anything about its history of occupation by Indonesia. An undoubted factor in making it known was the action of the four women who hammered the Hawk Ground Attack aircraft destined for sale to the Indonesian government. When the women were acquitted in a jury trial, the whole action exposed the cynicism of the arms sales to despotic regimes and our own government's involvement. Their actions are now even more vindicated in the light of recent events.

The case of nuclear weapons

We like to think that the U.K. is an open and democratic government, far above any direct forms of tyranny, but surely the fact that we hold the world in thrall under the threat of nuclear weapons is one of the most destructive and pervasive forms of tyranny we can imagine. Britain presently deploys four Trident nuclear submarines each carrying up to 48 warheads equivalent in destructive fire-power to eight times the Hiroshima bomb.

For most of my own campaigning life over the last twenty years I have been protesting against Trident nuclear submarines. I have used all the usual methods of raising the issue in public; speaking, lobbying, making exhibitions, marching, singing, letter-writing. But inevitably there comes a time when an issue is so passionately felt that civil disobedience seems the only option. In a seeming democracy, from a middle-class background, this is hard to do, but it is the logical and necessary next step in resisting oppression, and it is indeed the way in which most democratic change has come about. Always when taking such action one is concerned about the effects on public opinion. Will it alienate people; will one be branded as an extremist and lose all credibility? My experience is that the converse is true. When one takes action in conscience and is totally consistent and nonviolent, people do sit up and take notice, questions are asked and stereotypes broken in a way that genuinely works towards change.

However, direct action can also go far beyond the raising of public awareness in its effects. A vital element in nonviolent direct action is that it removes the fear surrounding authority, and enables people to take control of their own lives and destinies. There is a huge personal exhilaration in even the small symbolic act of cutting a military fence, disabling a weapons system, standing in front of a convoy of warheads. But the implications go far beyond personal gratification, important as that may be.

During the time of mass demonstrations in the 1980s, after years of lobbying and campaigning, the non-nuclear countries persuaded the

General Assembly of the U.N. to lay the question of the legality of nuclear weapons before the International Court of Justice in the Hague. In 1996 the Court gave its ruling that because of their indiscriminate nature weapons of mass-destruction were generally contrary to international humanitarian law, except for self-defence in times of extreme national emergency, and even then they still had to comply with humanitarian law. In effect they were ruled as illegal. As time went by, it became obvious that even with a change of government the U.K. was making no moves towards obeying this ruling, so a small group of activists formed a campaign known as Trident Ploughshares 2000. Some 200 people pledged to take direct action to disarm the weapons system in whatever way they could, openly, nonviolently and accountably. To date there have been over 300 court cases.

In June 1999 three women managed to climb onto a Trident related facility in Loch Goil in Scotland and threw the entire contents of a research laboratory to the bottom of the Loch. They were arrested and spent four and a half months in prison on remand. After a trial lasting almost five weeks, during which a great many expert witnesses were called, the judge gave the following ruling;

> The three took the view that if Trident is illegal, given the horrendous nature of nuclear weapons, they had the obligation in terms of international law to do whatever little they could to stop the deployment and use of nuclear weapons in situations which could be construed as a threat.

> It follows, if I consider that Angie Zelter, Ulla Roder and Ellen Moxley were justified in the first leg of their defence......that I will instruct the jury that they should acquit all three accused on the charges.[10]

The implications of this are recognised to be enormous, as the whole independence of the Scottish judiciary is called into question, causing a major constitutional crisis within the U.K. It is as if a huge stone has been removed from a river, and suddenly a rush of change is allowed to happen. Who knows where this action will end, but it has certainly challenged the very heart of the establishment in the U.K. A lead article in the Sunday Herald reported;

> The political and military establishment are seriously considering Sheriff Gimblett's ruling and the success of the Trident Ploughshares 2000 campaign...in scoring a victory which questions the legality of nuclear weapons.....Martin Butcher, a BASIC

Visiting Fellow in Washington, predicted the military
establishment would have to rethink its strategy on nuclear
deployment in the light of the Gimblett decision.[11]
Where the legal and military establishments are both major props in
the structure of the system, such results of a piece of creative direct
action are hugely encouraging.

We have been speaking in this book about nonviolent ways of resisting
oppression. When people are suffering the extremes of tyranny and
oppression in their own countries; where going to prison means torture
and disappearance, the least we can do to honour their courage is to be
prepared to risk a little ourselves by stepping out of line.

There is so much we can do at home on our own doorsteps to work
towards resisting tyranny and the prevention of deadly conflict, but
there is also a place for direct intervention. Much of this is already
going on, as Judith Large and Diana Francis describe in this book.
Over the past few years there has been a growing movement in several
countries, including Sweden, Germany, the U.S. and Scotland to form
international civilian peace teams, where thousands of well-trained,
well-prepared civilians would be part of a nonviolent stand-by unit
ready to go to an area of conflict at short notice.[12]

So often the nonviolent responses to violent conflict seem to be so
small and insignificant and too late. I firmly believe as we move into
the 21st century that there is a climate for change that is ready to look
for the nonviolent solutions. The year 2000 is the U.N. year for the
Culture of Peace and we enter the Decade for Building a Culture of
Nonviolence. We can make the difference in such a variety of small
ways that together add up to the paradigm shift that needs to happen.
The signs are already there. If we do not seize the opportunity now to
seek the alternatives, then the future is bleak indeed.

> We are now faced with the fact that tomorrow is today. There is
> such a thing as being too late. Over the bleached bones of
> numerous civilisations are written the pathetic words "too late". If
> we do not act, we shall surely be dragged down the dark corridors
> of time reserved for those who possess power without compassion,
> might without morality, and strength without sight.[13]
> (Martin Luther King)

References

1   Gene Sharp; *Social Power and Political Freedom* Porter Sargent, USA, 1976)
2   *Statement of Concerned Serbian Citizens*, (Belgrade, April 16 1999)
3   Gene Sharp; *ibid*
4   Martin Luther King; *Strength to Love* (Collins, 1984)
5   Hannah Arendt: *Eichman in Jerusalem: a report on the banality of evil.* (Penguin, 1994)
6   Elias Chacour; *Blood Brothers* (Kingsway, 1985)
7   "The Gulfwatch Papers" *Edinburgh Review* 1992
8   Quoted in *Quaker Faith and Practice* (Britain Yearly Meeting, 1994)
9   Gene Sharp; *ibid*
10 Sheriff Margaret Gimlett at Greenock Sheriff Court, Oct 1999 as reported by SCND
11 Quoted by David Hartsough in *Peaceworkers*, Sept 1994
12 Andrew Morton; *Civil Peace Service for Non-Military Conflict Handling* (Edinburgh, March 1996)
13 Martin Luther King: *ibid.*

PACIFISM AND THE REAL WORLD

Diana Francis

The continuous news from so many conflict areas may make us despair of ending war and repression. Diana Francis, a former President of the International Fellowship of Reconciliation, has visited many of these places to have dialogue with those caught up in war situations and to explore with them ways of building a better future. Here she explains why we should not give up hope.

Why were so many of us struck dumb (at least initially) by the war against Serbia? Why did we find it hard to speak out against the intensive bombing of another nation, without any declaration of war? Why did some of us actually support it, albeit miserably? Partly, I believe, because we were confronted with evidence of barbarities which needed to be stopped, because it was suggested that all else had failed and it was unbearable to know what was happening and to do nothing. But the widespread silencing of objection depended on a more general and permanent deception, a pernicious myth: the myth of the efficacy of violence. Clearly violence does have effects: those of harming and destroying. And these effects are relatively easily achieved. For example, a boy who has experienced in his life little beyond frustration and humiliation may, in a moment, start a fire which destroys his school; or in a few moments shoot several class mates. Or an alliance of countries, deploying massive weaponry, may destroy an unimaginable number of lives, laying waste vast tracts of countryside and devastating many cities. In so doing, they may end a particular episode of tyranny; but the result, with the same amount of destruction, could also be the triumph of tyranny, since in war it is might that is right, and a just cause does not guarantee victory. Whatever its outcome, the violence of war represents an accumulation and succession of tyrannies and atrocities which flout all the norms and values which those who go to war argue they mean to uphold.

The story of wars throughout the ages has been a story of the struggle for domination; a story of the untold suffering of combatants and non-combatants alike, in which outcomes are decided by a combination of luck and power; a story in which even

121

victories involve huge losses, misery and destruction. Yet somehow war has acquired a scarcely contested reputation for effectiveness. Nowadays it is presented as "the means of last resort", what we turn to "when all else fails" as if then we had something we could rely on. Within the myth of war, to see injustice happening and not to resort to war is to refuse to do what is obvious and right and bound to succeed. Maybe the myth takes its strength from our inability to accept the realities of the human condition, to bear the frustration of limited powers and the fact of vulnerability just as to burn down a school or shoot some classmates may feel better (much better) than remaining powerless.

How else can we explain that, in the face of the predictable calamity that would be precipitated by the bombing campaign launched against Serbia, the NATO governments went ahead? How else could it have seemed that making things unspeakably worse was better than doing nothing?

In the case of Kosov@, as in many other cases, the justification of war as the means of last resort was based on two false assumptions. The first was that all else really had been tried and the second that those other attempts had been proved conclusively to be without any hope of success or somehow rendered impossible to continue. In fact, very little had been done, and that belatedly, inadequately and ineptly (or disingenuously). The West had studiously ignored the sinister warnings that began in 1989, before war broke out in the Balkans, when Slobodan Milosevic used Kosov@ as a rallying cry for Serb nationalism in order to thrust himself into a position of political prominence and popularity. We continued to ignore the by now greatly intensified conflict and human rights violations in Kosov@ when we brokered the Dayton Agreement. Our only action until very shortly before the bombing of Serbia was its classification as a pariah state, the refusal of help for its massive refugee problem, and an extremely belated denunciation of the appalling treatment of Albanians in Kosov@, along with an insistence on the immutability of Serb borders. The more constructive move of sending Organisation for Security and Co-operation in Europe (OSCE) monitors into Kosov@ came very late, and the number of monitors actually sent was woefully inadequate, reflecting a lack of real commitment, as well as a lack of preparedness.

Instead of serious negotiations, what followed were the so-called "talks" at Rambouillet , in which terms were dictated which would inevitably be refused by Serbia (indeed, seemed designed to be so). And what forced the decision to abandon negotiations and start bombing was not some final proof of the impossibility of making progress by non-military means but a deadline which the NATO countries had imposed on themselves. By then there was a political "need" (and probably a psychological one) to act "decisively", to be seen to be in control. Threats of violence had to be carried out, to avoid humiliation, despite the warnings of military experts and despite the threats of Milosevic and his entourage to step up their assaults on Kosov@ Albanians if that were to happen. It was as if the police, in some siege in this country, were to open fire on a gunman who was holding a family hostage and threatening to kill them if he was attacked; but in such cases our police have learned to be patient, and to put the lives of hostages first. The art of skilled negotiation has been developed by the police, but not, apparently, by foreign secretaries; or maybe it is rather that foreign secretaries have additional agendas.

Ironically, the UK Government, while loudly endorsing the bombing of Serbia, was struggling to keep the Northern Ireland peace process on the road. In that case it had been decided that it was necessary, for the sake of all who live in Northern Ireland, to include "the men of violence" in the dialogue and to draw them into the political processes aimed towards peace. This was a courageous decision, taken in a context of competing moral demands. When it came to Milosevic, however, in the run up to the bombing, the implication of UK pronouncements was that it would be wrong to negotiate with a leader who was abusing his power, and principled and right to use overwhelming military advantage to bomb a wide range of targets in his country, inflicting widespread and longlasting misery on his people, even though the effect on those whose protection was at issue would be catastrophic.

It has been argued that since the overwhelming majority of Kosov@'s Albanian population who were the victims of Serb violence supported the bombing of Serbia (including their own part of it), that very fact justified the bombing. But that is like arguing that if a family who had seen one of its members murdered supported a lynching, the lynching would therefore be justified even if it was calculated to lead to a new and worse wave of murders. Albanian anger and the desire for revenge are certainly understandable. They do not, however, necessarily represent the best basis for moral or practical judgement, which must have been distorted by the horror and confusion of what was happening, as well as by resentments built up over many years of harassment and discrimination. If the order of events was soon forgotten in the NATO countries, and disguised in NATO presentations, it is not too surprising that it was obscured or forgotten in the midst of the misery and horror of the action. Most of us have probably, in less dire circumstances, succumbed to the feeling that "my enemy's enemy is my friend"; but it is not a sound principle for deciding and judging action.

What could have been done? Even within the range of conventional international relations, there were, at different points, many possibilities. In terms of the recent past, the needs of Kosov@ should have been addressed in the Dayton agreement, through guarantees for the human rights of minorities and the restoration of autonomy. Then, since the continuation of Milosevic in office was being accepted as a given, he could have been offered economic and political carrots in exchange for democratic reforms and improvements in the realm of human rights, instead of simply being punished and threatened with economic sticks and political opprobrium. At the same time, there could have been international support, both moral and practical, for the democracy movement in Serbia and for the nonviolent movement for Albanian rights in Kosov@, both of which were strong and courageous, but starved of support and encouragement and beset by internal divisions. Encouragement was therefore needed also for those groups in the region working at the educational level for humane approaches to intergroup relations, effective political participation and the constructive handling of conflict. And these things could have been done in the context of a process for the whole region of inclusion in the good things available to West Europeans, through membership of the European Union.

The notion of inclusion is fundamental in nonviolent approaches to conflict. It means that everyone in a situation of conflict is to be treated as if they were of value and as if they had legitimate needs which should be met. This is not only a profoundly important moral and philosophical commitment; it also represents a vital understanding of what is needed for relatively secure and efficient co-existence and co-existence is not an option, but a necessity. If any group is excluded from participation in society and its goods, it will find ways of making itself felt and meeting its needs, and those ways are unlikely to be in the best interests of the others. Societies (on whatever scale) which do not operate by consent are not safe or comfortable to live in. Violent social and political conflicts disrupt and obstruct all other efforts to meet human needs and further peaceable desires.

Even more seriously, the exclusion of some from the rights and protections of society undermines the very notion of human rights which can provide a basis for political and social arrangements worthy of the name of civilisation. Human rights are by nature unconditional. War (including any military intervention) means the suspension of the human rights of some, treating them as if they were no longer human, holding the right to life and dignity, no longer worthy of trial before execution. If we argue that some people forfeit their rights by their behaviour, we deny the very nature of human rights, which is that they depend on nothing, belonging as much to the most depraved of human beings as to a saint.

The philosophy of nonviolence presupposes not only the worth of all human beings, but also their responsibility to be active on each other's behalf. Inaction in the face of cruelty and injustice is not an option. This does not, however, imply that all suffering or all violence can be prevented; only that one should do everything possible and constructive to prevent it. Nonviolence does not allow for the demonising and punishment of whole nations. It does encourage courageous action, solidarity and strategic realism. Its object is not the glorification of politicians, but the wellbeing of people.

Most human interaction is, mercifully, not-violent, without being nonviolent in any positive, principled or conscious way, and there was much that could have been done by European governments to support advance towards human rights and democracy in Serbia and Kosov@ within the framework of current, mainstream norms. Although the nonviolent action of Serbs and Albanians to overthrow tyranny, in the face of internal divisions, international neglect and the intransigence and brutality of the Milosevic regime, was eventually submerged in violence, it was nonetheless deeply impressive, and in Serbia looks set to recover and continue. If we have any doubts about the potential of "people power", we should cast our minds back to the events of a decade ago, when what is now the post-communist world gave us the most dramatic, large-scale and successful examples since Gandhi of the power of unarmed and non-destructive action by ordinary people. Somehow we do not seem to have grasped the implications of what happened then. Such is the power of the military myth, that although we saw in daily, graphic detail on our television screens the overthrow of a mighty military empire by force of will and numbers, imagination and persuasion, rather than by violence, we still think of military force as the only kind that counts. Neither have we, it seems, absorbed the significance of the fact that, during the same half century, we have witnessed the humiliation of great military powers in Vietnam, Afghanistan and Iraq, where massive military onslaughts have produced not submission, but untold human suffering and defiance, and the continuation of political tyranny in one form or another.

In addition to these recent striking successes of nonviolent action and failures of militarism, a change in popular attitudes to war puts at issue the very basis of military intervention, at least in forms which would come anywhere near meeting "just war" criteria. There is increasing unwillingness within political constituencies to tolerate the loss of the lives of a country's own nationals in combat, at least where the combat is not immediately related to "the defence of the realm". The lives of NATO forces were in practice valued infinitely more highly than all others, whether Albanian or Serb, in the recent war. Everything was designed to preserve them, regardless of the cost to those on the ground. This meant that the requirement to protect civilian lives first and foremost was set aside and that in terms of the proclaimed aims of the intervention there was paralysis of all military muscles but one. Only the muscle for long range bombing was able to operate.

Not only have military methods of arranging human affairs proved enormously destructive and often impotent to achieve their declared objectives; there are so many bloody conflicts going on around the world that it is difficult to see them all being "solved" by the international community. The people whose lives are at stake cannot wait for others to liberate them. They need to discover and harness their own power to transform the societies in which they live, ensuring that their voices are heard and that they are active within their own spheres to shape relationships and events. Although so many regions are characterised by injustice and human rights abuses, there are also many examples of courage, determination and effective action which can lend inspiration to necessity. We must support and publicise such efforts and successes, and be part of a worldwide movement to encourage ordinary people (including ourselves) to assume responsibility for their own lives and take collective action, so that demagoguery and brutality do not hold sway unopposed, but the contexts in which they flourish are transformed from below.

According to Johan Galtung (1990), the direct violence of murder, imprisonment, starvation or "ethnic cleansing" happens not in a vacuum but within a context of both structural and cultural violence. Violent structures include the economic, political and military systems and relationships which oppress people and of which we are a part. Cultures of violence which justify them, and their enforcement through military domination, also justify the brutalisation of one ethnic group by another, the exploitation and abuse of children by their elders, and the treatment of women as men's chattels. In the UK, the dominant culture, which perpetuates the myth of the morality and effectiveness of war, makes acceptable our possession of weapons of mass destruction and recently justified a massive assault on another nation, involving a large number of civilian deaths and causing great and prolonged hardship and pollution. If we are to halt the terrible episodes of cruelty which disfigure our world, we shall have to change radically the prevailing cultures and distorting structures which blight our current global society and societies, embodying, motivating and justifying brutal disregard for the lives and rights of human beings.

In the meantime there are circumstances, like those in East Timor, in which, because of past disregard and collusion from outside, the role of external vested interests and the cruelty and disarray of powerholders in the region, an extreme humanitarian crisis has arisen which calls for urgent action. What can be done in such circumstances? Sometimes we may have to accept that once the dynamic of violence has accelerated to a certain point, nothing on earth can instantly stop it, though they may add to it. This is not to say that all efforts should be suspended, but that the longer a mounting crisis has been ignored, the less likely it becomes that widescale bloodshed can be averted. If such tragedies and enormities are to be prevented, a major shift in international priorities will be required: a shift from barely adulterated self-interest to a real commitment to global responsibility; to a genuine sense of human equality, which values the lives and needs of those of other cultures and in other lands as highly as those of one's own place and background; which puts the welfare of all in an interdependent world before the ever-increasing wealth of a minority. Lip-service to "early warning" must be replaced by a real readiness for early action, in support of local initiatives, along with a fundamental change in attitudes, lifestyles and priorities.

Such a shift in thinking and values would, in turn, persuade our leaders that they could no longer justify the mass production and export of arms of all kinds, no longer see them as a means of making money, but recognise their true nature as instruments of human destruction and bringers of death. Although the absence of arms will not alone prevent murder, even on a wide scale, a sharp decrease in the availability of arms and the changed attitudes it signified would reduce the likelihood and intensity of armed violence and change the climate which makes it an ever-present option.

My argument is that a trend towards more vigilant, compassionate and unselfish involvement in world affairs, a more lively sense of responsibility for the well-being of others, including the will to prevent outbreaks of killing and "ethnic cleansing", will happen, if at all, in the context of a general awakening of moral concern. Maybe the world's anguish at events in Kosov@ and East Timor is a sign of a growing sense of co-responsibility, even though the international response has been both slow and, in the first case at least, tragically and massively violent and counterproductive. Maybe from now on there will be more willingness to pre-empt widescale violence by constructive pressure, support, encouragement and example, so that we are not left with the impossible task of trying to prevent orgies of killing once they are under way. And such a change in climate would, in turn, bring new openness to forms of intervention which also embody and uphold respect for human life.

Till recently, despite the failure of militarism to provide an antidote to human cruelty, the idea of nonviolent intervention has been regarded with much scepticism and indeed, in the past, has been considered fanciful, or not considered at all. On a small scale, the nonviolent accompaniment of threatened groups and individuals, for instance by members of Peace Brigades International (PBI) in Guatemala and Sri Lanka, has a proven track record. PBI teams have accompanied those working for peace and human rights, so offering them some protection. The constant, vigilant, unarmed presence of foreign nationals has made a difference. It has required training and considerable courage on the part of the volunteers who have done the accompanying—just as soldiers have to be trained and courageous.

The Balkans Peace Team has developed this kind of small scale, civilian volunteer work, and has been taken seriously enough to receive funding from such bodies as the UK Department for International Development. It was formed in 1993 by a coalition of peace organisations, in response to the situation then pertaining in Kosov@. Its purpose was to offer the service of small, international teams of trained volunteers, who could support and facilitate the work of local individuals and groups working for the nonviolent transformation of the conflict affecting them. They were to act as channels for information and communication both on the ground and with supportive organisations outside the region. Teams have been located at different times in Croatia, Serbia, Macedonia and now in Kosov@. They have served as international eyes on what was happening, for example being present at trials or at threatened house evictions. They have convened gatherings of activists, (re)established connections with and between those displaced by war and helped forge links between those working on similar issues in different parts of the region. The team currently located in Pristina is providing a vital contact point in circumstances where communication can be very difficult and information is suppressed. It hopes to provide an unthreatening focus for the rebuilding of contact between divided communities, to begin with in one small town. It has also helped facilitate the dialogue with other organisations.

So far, such efforts have been few and small, and peace teams of this kind have had to struggle for funding. They have therefore not been able to have an impact on a wider scale. But the principle of their role, which is to support local initiatives, provides a sound basis for development. With substantial political and financial support their effect could be considerable. There is, of course, a danger that an enthusiasm for intervention could in practice undermine the will and efforts of local people, and constitute a new form of old colonialisms.

The only legitimate role for outsiders to a situation is in helping to provide a space in which local forces for peace and social organisation can recover and assume responsibility. Although such supportive interventions had till very recently been small in scale and marginal in terms of official politics, in the last few years, in the "real world" of European politics at the governmental level, the OSCE has begun to play such a role through human rights monitoring and mediation. The effectiveness of even the pathetically small team of OSCE monitors deployed in Kosov@ was demonstrated, alas, negatively, by the instant increase in barbarities when they were withdrawn. Had they been well trained and resourced, and deployed in the numbers intended (or more), their positive impact could have been expected to be much greater. In order to test the effectiveness of non-military intervention forces, we would need governments who would give them substantial funds, training, logistical support and credibility. We would need to overcome the argument of "it's never been done" by encouraging the realisation that it could be.

Since we have no experience of the deployment of unarmed intervention forces on a large scale, we can only speculate as to their impact. I believe that they would need to be clearly civilian, international, and free of vested interest or long term ambitions in the region, in order to have legitimacy and the kind of psychological effect which could change the dynamics of hostility. At present any large scale mobilisation of civilians for unarmed intervention is outside the scope of mainstream political imagination; but we do have the OSCE experiences to build on, which could help the imaginative climate to change and increase our understanding of just what works and how, and of the necessary preparations and logistics.

We also need to build our understanding of what makes the acceptance of such interventions more or less likely. For instance, if a political leader can see some possible advantage from co-operation with such an intervention and from giving way to international demands and norms, he or she will be far more likely to agree to it than if it comes as part of a package of public threats and humiliation. If it is felt to be just another form of bullying by those who traditionally call the global shots, it will be resisted, and rightly so. Hostility within Indonesia to the Australian-led intervention into East Timor bodes ill for the future of the region. It will be vital that control is returned rapidly to local people; but a peace that is built on military force will be fragile and, very likely, militarily dependent. Any intervention designed to make space for local peace capacities should be conducted in a way that not only is seen to be so but does so at every stage.

Maybe the climate change needed has already begun. We have a government in the UK which supports conflict resolution work through its Department for International Development, and funds the training of that department's staff in constructive approaches to conflict. This new element of policy in a government department, like the efforts being made for peace in Northern Ireland, reflects a growing understanding that violence can and must be addressed constructively and at every level; that the systemic violence of poverty and exclusion needs to be tackled at its roots; that wars constitute in themselves the biggest single cause of poverty and human rights violations, and that the building of peaceable relationships is a developmental rather than a military matter.

We now have a government committed to developing "an ethical foreign policy". Measuring the things that have been done against the claims that have been made, it is easy to feel cynical. But even broken promises of this kind are a sign of a shift in the moral ground we have to stand on as a society. Is it inconceivable to think that some time in the future the Foreign Office will call in conflict resolution experts to help them think constructively about the many wars in the making which are brewing (often with our help) in different parts of the world, including our own?

For now, we have to recognise that because of prevailing traditions, practices and structures, catastrophes are happening which cannot all be prevented. It is therefore our job not to despair, but also not to be drawn into the perpetuation of that reality, but rather to work to change it, accepting that it cannot be transformed in an instant and that in the meantime we have no choice but to be caught up in the suffering and to share in the sense of helplessness. We cannot escape, but we can, in Martin Luther King's words, "keep our eyes on the prize".

That prize, I believe, is not some final escape from human frailty and destructiveness, and certainly not an end to all suffering. It is a radical cultural change, across our shrinking planet, in which, in the words of the Hague Appeal for Peace, war is delegitimised, and we escape from the illusion of the separation between processes and outcomes, recognising that we cannot fight fire with fire, create trust through terror, teach gentleness by beating, human rights by bombing or respect by humiliation. The prize will be an understanding that an act of love, just like an act of hate, is in itself an outcome of something else, and will have its own repercussions.

If we want to keep our eyes on the prize, we must work creatively in the gap between the world as it is and the world as we want it to be, exploring the application of methods and values of a very different kind in the presence of existing norms and practices. We need to learn from all the experiments and experience which are being built up in nonviolent, constructive approaches to conflict, to document and publicise them. We need to work to introduce and develop these approaches in our education systems and in popular culture. We need to ensure that those of us who have some influence in policy-making circles (academics, for instance) seek out every opportunity to meet with MPs, government members, party leadership, civil servants and the like. We must challenge and supplant the idea that national self-interest is the most appropriate basis for foreign policy (perhaps challenge the notion of foreign policy itself). We must support organisms designed to promote the ideas of mutual support and responsibility among all people, particularly the UN (albeit in need of radical reform) and, within Europe, the OSCE. We must praise constructive, ethical actions and policies of governments and build on them as growing points, while at the same time identifying and challenging contradictions.

We can help promote new perspectives that can change reality. We can refuse all ideologies of separation, all "us and them talk", all categorisations which dehumanise and belittle others. We can participate in a process of rethinking in relation to national identities and the meaning of democratic pluralism, asking ourselves and others how best to hold together the human needs of identity and security, how to find forms of belonging which do not lead to patterns of exclusion. This will entail a rejection of nationalism, old and new, and a fundamental challenge to current thinking about states, since state nationalism and militarism have till now been bound together, war being the system on which states and notions of nationhood were built.

We can refuse the "might is right" paradigm; refuse also the "need" to have more power than others and know best for everyone, while ignoring our own part in injustice and violence. We can acknowledge the cruelties and inadequacies of the past, both communist and capitalist, religious and secular, recognising that we need to rethink our relationships to each other and to the planet we inhabit. We can accept both our limitations and our potential as human beings: our mortality, vulnerability and interdependence—and develop a culture and a politics based on the idea of human community rather than contest, of co-operation rather than domination (Eisler, 1990). There will never be a good time to give up war, and it will not be abolished over night. The cultural and systemic changes which are needed for us to recover and grow beyond our dependence on violence will take time. But for the move to happen at all, war needs, in the words of the Hague Appeal for Peace, to be "delegitimised". That means that those of us who see that the human and ecological costs of war are morally untenable must continue to say so; for the moral cost of war is the denial and erosion of the only values which could ever justify it.

All of us can act in some way, and the most important place to start is with our own thinking and speaking. We can stop apologising for our rejection of violence, and refuse the fatalism of there will always be wars. The future will be what we make it.

Riane Eisler: *The Chalice and the Blade: Our History, Our Future.* (London: Unwin Paperbacks, 1990.)

Johan Galtung: "Cultural Violence". *Journal of Peace Research*, vol. 27, no.3, 1990, pp. 291—305.

NOT TOO LATE TO LEARN

Paul Oestreicher

And so to the end of history, murder shall breed murder, always in the name of right and honour and peace, until at last the gods tire of blood and create a race that can understand.

G.B. Shaw: *Caesar & Cleopatra*

Will history end first or will the false gods of our civilization tire of blood before it's too late? The taste of blood is too intoxicating. We cannot afford to leave the world's fate in the hands of the deities of wealth, power and privilege. I was thirteen when we entered the nuclear age, a schoolboy in New Zealand when, with a USAF chaplain's prayers, the crew set off for Hiroshima. There was no soft-soap-talk of possible collateral damage. This was death to perfection at the press of a button. But still small scale: just one whole city at a time.

The next morning our physics teacher tried to explain to us what had happened. I was never any good at physics but I cannot forget his words as the lesson ended; "Boys, either we now learn to abolish war, or war will abolish us."

Half a century has passed. That isn't long. For a few thousand years bows and arrows and slings were all that technology could offer. But from the gun to the possibility of bacteriological wipeout has been a very short time. Technology now moves much faster than our human capacity to change. Collectively, we still live in the era of the crusades.

For Margaret Thatcher the Falklands campaign was a holy war, as Kosovo has just been for Tony Blair. Winning proves we must be morally right (though God is now less often called in aid) and it is all hugely popular. No difference there between British and Russian sentiment in Chechnya. Losing is different. Hitler's generals beamed as they conquered Europe, and sent the brilliant Rommel to take Africa as well. The more intelligent of them turned on their master, too late, when it all went sour.

Pacifist that I am both as a would-be follower of Jesus of Nazareth and as a child of the Enlightenment, I have great respect for the formulation of the doctrine of the just (though justifiable is a better word) war.   It is the only theologically legitimate doctrine apart from its even better alternatlve, pacifism. They are not all that far apart.

The conditions that are said to make a war just, both in its declaration and in its subsequent pursuit, are spelt out by Elizabeth Salter on page 42. They are so stringent that hardly any war actually conforms to them. If Christians and society really accepted the just war doctrine more widely, then de-facto pacifism would be the norm and the resort to violence the barely conceivable exception.

What desperately needs curing, personally and collectively, is the deep instinct to retaliate at any cost as a moral obligation: the spirit of crusade.   In every British war cemetery the sword is superimposed on the cross. The Germans, through two world wars, wrote "God with us" on their belt-buckles. Britons would not be so crass as to so parade the obvious. The Americans, with a finer sense of what is holy, engrave their trust in God on their coinage.

Thomas Mann came close to the truth when he wrote that "war is a coward's escape from the problems of peace."   The analyses in this book by Judith Large and Diana Francis of the NATO action against Serbia illustrate that well. The politicians chose what they thought would be a relatively painless short-cut. In fact it was a disaster and very far from a victory for human rights. The month I spent in Belgrade after the bombing convinced me of that. The coolest advocate of *realpolitlk*, Henry Kissinger, analyzed this better than any pacifist in *Newsweek*. It is not really strange, how much more clearly politicians out of power can see reality, than those who have to act and are afraid to think new thoughts. Power not only corrupts, it tends to paralyse.

There is no fundamental difference between persons individually and collectively. Niebuhr's belief in *Moral Man and Immoral Society* (the title of his best-known work) is mistaken. He held collective goodness to be misguided romanticism and therefore war to be a necessary and inevitable evil. If he is right, then the human family has no long-term future. I put my faith in the possibility that he is wrong. Sin is real but its conquest must be possible. That calls for a new collective mind-set and better structures for peace.

All is not bleak on the peace front, though it is still far from where pacifists would like it to be. It may not be too late. The serious study of peace now rivals the much more traditional study of war. Bodies of law—though still not widely respected—now exist, which outlaw all manner of violence snd create the beginnings of internatlonal enforce-ment angencies, as Bernard Hamilton explains. National sovereignty, the cause of so much conflict, is no longer sacrosanct.

Most significantly, armed forces are beginning to be seen not as instru-ments of national power (very tentative beginnings) but as police forces under supra-national control to stop wars or to prevent them from breaking out. Like policemen, the soldiers will have failed in their task if they resort to using their arms. That is still several steps removed from the unarmed, well-trained peace corps that is the ideal. It is no more than a step in the right direction, but an important one, even though it too is open to abuse when there is a hidden political agenda. There are senior soldiers today who understand the need for peace better than many politicians who still regard war as a continuation of politics by other means; consider Kosovo again. As we enter the third millennium I have become convinced that Jesus (and Gandhi and Martin Luther King) were realists. War is no longer an enlightened option. The theologian in me and the political scientist now inhabit the same ground.

If I am right, I have no need to make a fetish of the word *pacifist*, not if it inhibits the educative process that Einstein recognised to be a leap of consciousness greater than any revolution in the natural sciences. It really is about creating the "single new humanity" that St Paul saw foreshadowed in the life and death and resurrection of Jesus.

We must find our allies in the search for this breakthrough where we can. Organised religion may help and may equally well hinder. Fortunately, the inoculation of religion is no certain protection against holiness. The Bird of Heaven, God's free spirit, is not likely to be caged up in any holy shrine—but may freely choose to rest awhile even there. And in this context, what I am talking about (like Helen Steven) is holy disobedience, the rejection of a mind-set as old as the common life of human beings.

That Coventry's very secular university should have set up a Centre for the Study of Forgiveness and Reconciliation in the School of Law and Politics, headed by a committed pacifist, is not yet a copernican revolu-tion, but a hint at its possibility. There are more lights in the darkness than we see at first glance, but the darkness is real.

If "our earthly condition is essentially that of wayfarers, of incomplete-ness moving towards fulfilment, and therefore of struggle" (Yves Congar), then we need each other in the otherwise too lonely struggle. Daniel Berrigan wrote in good humour from an American prison, during the struggle against the Vietnam War, that "unless the cries of the war victims, the hopeless poor, the resisters of conscience—unless the cry of the world—reaches our ears, nothing changes, least of all ourselves; we stand like sticks and stones, impervious to the meaning of history or the cry of its Lord and Victim."

NOTES ON CONTRIBUTORS

Michael Bartlet is a lawyer and teacher who currently works as Parliamentary Liaison Officer for Britain Yearly Meeting of the Religious Society of Friends.

Kevin Clements is Secretary General of International Alert in London and Professor of Conflict Resolution at George Mason University, USA. He has been Head of the Peace Research Institute at Australian National University; President of the International Peace Research Association and Secretary General of the Asia Pacific Peace Research Association. He and his wife Valerie were Quaker Representatives in Geneva in the 1980s and he was Assistant Clerk of Friends World Committee soon after that. A sociologist and political scientist by training, most of his writing has been in the area of development, peace, conflict transformation and security issues and he has written or edited five books and over 130 academic articles on these topics.

Diana Francis is a pacifist Quaker with a campaigning background. During her eight years as President of the International Fellowship of Reconciliation she had the opportunity to travel widely and learn about nonviolence in action. For the last ten years or so, she has worked for a variety of organisations in many countries, facilitating workshops for training and dialogue in situations of interethnic conflict.

Bernard F. Hamilton is the President of the Leo Kuper Foundation, which works for the eradication of genocide. He is an experienced human rights advocate who has worked in Washington, Geneva and London. He has published widely in the field of international law. He teaches international criminal law and human rights law at the University of London.

Peter Jarman is Clerk of Quaker Social Action that seeks to alleviate poverty in East London; Secretary of the Churches Human Rights Forum of Britain and Ireland, and the director of the ethics of sanctions study group of the Council on Christian Approaches to Defence and Disarmament. He is also a member of the Balkans mitigation team of the Transnational Foundation for Peace based in Sweden working in war torn regions of former Yugoslavia.

Roswitha Jarman, of German parentage, is a counselling psychologist and like Peter is engaged in conflict resolution work in the Former Soviet Union where they were Quaker representatives from 1991 to 1994. She currently works with a Dutch organisation in supporting the peoples of Chechnya and adjacent regions of the North Caucasus.

John Lampen with his wife Diana lived and worked for peace in Northern Ireland for eleven years. They played a significant role in starting peace education in schools in Belarus, Ukraine and Uganda. They have also worked in South Africa (during and after apartheid), Bosnia, Croatia and the Northern Caucasus.

Judith Large is an independent practitioner in conflict analysis and strategy formation who has worked with relief, development and peace NGOs, local groups and U.N. agencies in Croatia, Serbia, Bosnia, and Kosovo. She is currently committed to ongoing projects in conflict zones in Uganda and Indonesia. Judith convenes a course for the University of Kent's London Centre of International Relations in Applied Peacebuilding and Conflict Resolution. Author of *The War Next Door.*

Paul Oestreicher, Anglican priest and Quaker, was until recently Director of International Ministry at Coventry Cathedral. He is a former chairman of Amnesty International UK, and author of *The Double Cross.*

John Pilger is a war correspondent, film maker and playwright, who has won numerous rewards for his work, including "International Reporter of the Year" and the United Nations Association Media Peace Prize. He made the film *Year Zero: the Silent Death of Cambodia* which exposed the horrors of the Khmer Rouge regime, and *Death of a Nation: the Timor Conspiracy.* His books include *Heroes, A Secret Country, Distant Voices* and *Hidden Agendas.*

Elizabeth Salter has been Moderator of the Division of International Affairs at the British Council of Churches, and a member of the Commission of the Churches on International Affairs (CCIA) at the World Council of Churches. She joined the CCIA staff in 1990, travelling widely on peace-building missions, and eventually becoming responsible for setting up the WCC's Programme to Overcome Violence. In retirement she chairs the Churches Peace Forum.

SEZAM is a group of ten people based in Zenica, Bosnia. They work in local schools with children traumatised by war and returning refugee children.

Helen Steven is currently working at the new Scottish Centre for Nonviolence in Dunblane. She has been actively engaged in nonviolent protest and education for the past twenty years. Talks, lectures and workshops have taken her to such widely diverse places as the U.N. Peacekeeping Training Institute in Canada, NATO HQ in Brussels, and Cornton Vale Women's Prison.

Philip Wilkinson OBE is a Colonel in the Royal Artillery and is currently Assistant Director for Peace Support Operations at the army's new Joint Doctrine & Concepts Centre at Shrivenham. He has served with Commandos, Parachute Brigades and Special Forces. He has operational experience in the Far and Middle East, Central America, the Falklands, the Balkans and Northern Ireland. He has been responsible for military doctrine for Peace Support operations since 1993.